# HOW TO EXTEND YOUR HOME

## And get it right first time

Deepak Singh Udassi

Author's website: architecture100.com

Editing by Ilsa, WordSure Ltd

Book design by Helen, Jet the Dog



Paperback ISBN: 978-1-7396506-0-5

eBook ISBN: 978-1-7396506-1-2

# CONTENTS

# FOREWORD

I first met Deepak at a trade conference in 2018, where I was delivering a keynote speech on the UK construction sector. It was clear that Deepak and business partner Kuly are driven by a desire to raise standards and make house building an overall more pleasant experience for homeowners.

I too come from a background in construction, so architecture and building are close to my heart and I appreciate the challenges faced by the industry. It's often the outsider who has the ability to spot flaws in accepted wisdom and devise and implement the necessary fixes – Deepak does just that.

Since being elected as Member of Parliament in 2017, I have been a vocal advocate for UK construction. This is a topic so many people can relate to, and know the importance of responsible and professional housebuilding, having for example seen some of the excellent work done in Slough.

This book shines a light on the workings of residential design and build, and should be compulsory reading for consumers serious about renovating and extending their home, and indeed for any professionals working within the industry.

Rt Hon. Tan Dhesi

Member of Parliament

# PREFACE

Great. Another book on home improvement by another guy who thinks he knows what he's talking about.

However, this it isn't just another book. It is the book – the only book you need to read if you're thinking of extending your home.

Before you start, it will help if you know what qualifies me to write this book and why you should listen to what I have to say.

My journey was part planned, part serendipity ...

There are dozens of memories I cherish from my childhood, in particular of my Pops, and the best memories tend to involve him cursing with gusto in Pinglish (half English, half Punjabi). One example is the time Jacob the carpenter made a total hash of building an airing cupboard in the back bedroom of our Victorian terraced home. It was butchery of the highest level – you had a sense the cupboard would collapse under the slightest duress, and the hinges were kept in place by duct tape! But after he'd finished, Pops smiled, politely thanked him for his time and paid in full all the same. The aphorism 'Sala, Jacooob ... bloody sala ...' was repeated in our house for weeks after.

I read systems science at one of Europe's top business schools, where I learned the skill of breaking complex problems down into processes, boxes, arrows and variables, before reconstructing them all into a beautiful, better whole. This knack provided me with sufficient razzle dazzle to talk my way onto the graduate programme of one of Britain's biggest blue chips, where I plied my craft in high-intensity project management. There I witnessed first-hand the operational silliness that only dogmatic departmentalisation can bring. For example, spending entire mornings planning for meetings about planning with department heads and IT folk seemed plain stupid. We were all seated within 30 paces of each other so could just have converged at the coffee machine within seconds to get things drawn up, done and signed off.

The UK property market in 2006 wasn't just hot – it was sizzling. It felt like everyone was making a mint in the property market; banks were dishing out 110% mortgages like confetti ... and I wanted a slice of the action. So off I went to learn the property game, where for 18 months I laboured (often unpaid) on construction sites, sucking in every morsel of experience I could about how to develop property. I even qualified as a heating engineer and energy assessor along the way.

That was all fine until the subprime bubble burst in 2007, and the property market went from sizzling hot to fried to a crisp overnight. At that point, the only sensible move for me was to apply my nascent construction skills in the real world (or what was left of it) and get building.

By good fortune I had amassed a number of contacts via my surveying work, and through them I entered the property maintenance sector, before rolling on to small refurbishment jobs and then larger building projects. Over the next decade, my childhood friend, Kuly Sanghera, and I created a prosperous home extensions company. Kuly remains the single most gifted builder I have known, and with talent like that, everything is possible. In our pomp we completed over 50 extensions in a single year. And we collected a small arsenal of industry gongs along the way, culminating in our being crowned Britain's Most Heavenly Builder by the Federation of Master Builders (FMB) in 2019.

We were regularly handed poorly designed plans to build from by clients who knew no better, so out of necessity my role morphed into that of quasi designer-come-surveyor. Drawings in breach of planning rules, cut-and-paste structural detail, windows overlooking bins, foundations in neighbouring properties – you name it, we saw it. The progression to establishing our fully fledged architectural practice, architecture100.com, was therefore both natural and necessary, for our clients to avoid the despair of poorly executed home improvement projects.

I have been the duped customer, the thoughtful designer and the hands-on builder. This 360-degree endowment brings with it the same big-picture perspective usually enjoyed by fresh eyes, before experience displaces enterprise with acceptance.

In this book I share with you the benefit of my huge range of experiences so that you can avoid the nightmarish misery of a home improvement gone wrong.

By shining a light onto the workings of the home renovation industry, and onto the mechanisms of the home extension sector in particular, this book will help save homeowners from the agony of renovation nightmares.

You will learn why so many home extensions end in failure. You will discover the straightforward, step-by-step process you need to follow in order to minimise the chances of your home improvement going wrong. And you will understand how to get the most out of each stage of the process, so at the end you are left with a stunning extension built on time, on specification and on budget. Your home 2.0.

## WE BRITS LOVE EXTENDING

It's no surprise that the home renovation and extension sector is booming. In 2014 stamp duty was jacked up, which raised the cost of upsizing to a larger property. At the time of writing, according to the UK government's house price index, the average price of a typical semi-detached in London is £780,500 With stamp duty at 5%, owners of a typical semi-detached in London would pay an eye-watering £19,200 in tax for the privilege of moving house – enough to make a serious dent in the cost of any house extension. Meanwhile, money has never been cheaper, the interest rate in England standing at a historic low. High street banks are falling over themselves, clambering to lend their money to low-risk homeowners with low-rate remortgage products.

Oddly, property prices remain high, despite the 2007–08 financial crisis and the battering sterling took in the wake of Brexit, and even after the 2020–22 pandemic. In fact, in many parts of the country the cost of improvements actually pay for themselves on account of surging asset values post-extending.

With the liberalisation of planning rules following Prime Minister Boris Johnson's 'build build build' drive in June 2020, which (on paper) allowed homeowners to build bigger with fewer barriers, the decision to extend has never been easier.

In 'Hiscox Renovations and Extensions Report 2018', the insurer reports that Britain is officially becoming a nation of home improvers, with the number of planning applications submitted rocketing by 29% compared with a decade ago. Indeed, in some parts of the UK, close to one in three people decided to renovate and extend rather than move. This home improvement trend is further corroborated by Money.com, who reported in 'The 2020 Renovation Nation Report' that a whopping 65% of homeowners invested in some form of home improvement during and resulting from 2020–21 pandemic lockdowns. In fact, in 2021 a record 723,552 planning applications were submitted through the Planning Portal, which was largely driven by home improvement projects.

**In the five years to May 2019, 110,000 extensions were built in Britain under the permitted development pathway alone. That's a new extension starting every 24 minutes!**

*DIY Week* published a report in 2020, the name of which corroborates this home extension boom: 'Half of Brits set to spend £47 billion on home improvements in 2021'. Many other sources claim even higher figures.

Unfortunately, the labour supply required to service this growing demand has not kept pace – a problem compounded by the drain of skilled labour following Britain's departure from the EU. As there are virtually no barriers to entering the building industry, the risk of rogues and rookies entering the marketplace is huge, as is the potential for any project to go pear-shaped.

James and Emma's extension was supposed to cost £65,000.

In the end it cost them the princely sum of £86,000.

They had lived with their two daughters in their end-of-terrace home for five years. As the family grew, so did their need for space. The family were desperate for a second bathroom as well as a dedicated office for James, who worked from home as an IT consultant.

James and Emma did the maths and concluded it would be cheaper to extend their current house than to move to a larger one. They invited a builder to give an estimate for a side extension, and they applied to remortgage their property to cover the cost of work. They even drew down a little extra for an overdue family holiday.

But James and Emma hadn't accounted for the cost of difficult neighbours. Or for the necessity of an architect or engineer. Also, the need for a more powerful boiler or electrical upgrades wasn't made clear to them. And they assumed the cost of bathroom fitting and decorating was included ... but it was not.

They were forced to borrow from the bank of mum and dad, and they took out a very expensive personal loan to cover the shortfall.

To cap it all off, their daughters weren't at all happy that their long-awaited week in the Caribbean was downgraded to a weekend in Weymouth.

Does James and Emma's story sound familiar? It's likely you've heard similar. Regrettably, this sort of scenario plays out in home after home across the country. The demand for home improvements has never been higher, yet consumer awareness of the full extent of the home renovation process is worryingly low.

**The purpose of this book is to save homeowners like you from the nightmare of a home improvement going wrong.**

# THE BASICS

'Home improvement' is a catch-all term, covering everything from a 15-minute paint job to a 15-month total do-over. For the purposes of this book, a home improvement will refer exclusively to a home extension. 'Renovation' is equally nebulous, so again we refer to it here only in the context of extensions.

> **An extension is the permanent addition of some form of new space to an existing residential property.**

Extensions come in many forms:

- Single or double side extensions
- Single or double rear extensions
- Garage conversions
- Conservatories and orangeries
- Loft extensions
- Lean-to and infill extensions
- Wraparounds
- Piggyback extensions
- Porches
- First-floor extensions
- Granny annexes and other outhouses
- Roof gardens
- Any combination of the above

This book does not cover new builds, house-to-flat conversions, HMOs, mercantile-to-abode conversions or basement excavations. All of those require special considerations of their own, although the lessons you'll learn here would still apply.

This isn't a technical manual on how to renovate your home. It is a powerful guide that untangles the chaotic and frenzied activities involved in extending a home, arranging them in a clear and precise process. This will take you from the moment you first conceive the idea of extending, all the way through to you enjoying your finished new space.

Each stage of the process is laid out in the order in which events unfold, and I'll share my top tips for making the entire process as effective as it can be.

# WHY HOME EXTENSIONS FAIL

***'Give me six hours to chop down a tree and I will spend the first four sharpening the axe.'*** *Abraham Lincoln*

In following this step-by-step process, you will tick every box needed to make your project a success and minimise the risk of making expensive mistakes along the way.

The process of extending your home isn't quantum mechanics. It is pretty straightforward and follows a logical flow. But if it's so uncomplicated, why do so many home improvements the length and breadth of Britain end in abject misery?

There are a whole heap of reasons, and every industry professional will have their own views. However, experience reveals that the drivers behind project failure tend to fall into one of two groups:

## 1. Lack of accountability in a disjointed system

Here's the thing: there is nobody actually in charge of your project. No maestro conducting the orchestra. And no single authority responsible for delivering your project on budget, on specification and on time. It's on you to ensure you keep your finger on the pulse, hire the right people and make the correct decisions.

Think about that. You are about to make a milestone decision in your life, with a massive price tag to boot. It will change the way you and your family live your lives, and there is nobody to manage the journey. It's like hitchhiking around the country without a map and relying on the goodwill of strangers to get you from one place to another.

One of the overriding problems is that homeowners start their home extension hegiras at different junctures. For some people, a chat with a builder friend is the first port of call. Others have the end product in mind and head straight down to the designer kitchen showroom, credit card in hand. But a lack of thorough planning puts homeowners at risk of missing critical aspects of the project.

Consider supermarkets, which by design always have single entrance points. This forces shoppers to start their shop in a systemised way, walking through carefully curated aisles, designed to optimise movement and reduce the risk of customers missing items off their shopping lists. Now imagine a supermarket with seven entrances, with no way to control customers' shopping journeys. At best, they'd be back and forth around the aisles like a frenzied pinball; at worse, customers would need to make return trips for the things they missed the first time around. The home extension process is no different.

The biggest difficulty with home extensions is that the whole system is disjointed. Key contributors in the process have their own ways of working, often doing so in disconnected silos, and as a result they can struggle to appreciate the project in its entirety.

Let's meet the key people who will be involved in creating your home extension.

### The architect

Plans for and designs the extension according to the client's brief, planning rules and building regulations.

Note: Not all residential architects are the same. Some may prefer to specialise in just one aspect of the process such as obtaining planning permission, so it is common for this role to be split between two or more professionals.

### The planning officer

Assesses the proposed scheme for compliance with the planning rules, with a view to granting or refusing planning permission.

### The structural engineer

Produces the structural calculations and resulting structural design for the extension.

Can also (where required) assess the structural integrity of the property as a means of baselining – checking that the condition of the property is kosher – before any plans and/or physical work are carried out.

### The party wall surveyor

Where the extension is notifiable under the 1996 Party Wall etc Act, the party wall surveyor serves notice(s) of planned works to adjoining owners; works to protect parties against malicious claims; and facilitates dispute resolution between neighbours, if required.

### The builder

Builds the extension for an agreed sum, according to the plan provided, and working to an agreed timeline.

### The building control inspector

Inspects building work for compliance with the minimum required regulatory standards, culminating in the issuing of a building works completion certificate.

### The homeowner

Is responsible for setting a clear design brief and for agreeing project costs and specifications with relevant parties and, of course, paying.

Note: There could well be additional stakeholders, depending on the circumstances of your case. These might include a separate CAD technician, multiple architects tackling different aspects of the planning application and design, a measuring surveyor, a quantity surveyor, project managers (which are often found with design and build suppliers and are sometimes project managers in name only), a planning appeals officer, and your neighbours (although this aspect is partly covered by the party wall surveyor). All these stakeholders represent extra links in the chain, further conflicting priorities and more pitfalls to swerve. They have been omitted from the main list above because the scope of this book focuses on a 'typical' residential project, where functions such as these are rolled into others or are simply not required.

All of the key people listed above – plus you, the reader – are specialists, and their/your knowledge and contributions rarely cross disciplines. However, successfully designing and building an extension necessitates simple and unconfused conversations between you all.

The following example demonstrates the problem.

> Marie has long dreamt of building a room in the attic of her three-storey townhouse, with large panoramic windows giving her unblemished vistas over London at sunset.
>
> Her architect dutifully ingested the design brief and successfully obtained planning permission for a stunning loft extension, with a jaw-dropping wall-to-wall, ceiling-to-floor bifolding door opening onto a Juliet balcony, precisely as Marie wanted.
>
> Marie jumped onto Pinterest and found the exact set of bifolds she wanted – a four-panel, gunmetal-grey, powder-coated unit,

finished with a single piece of glass for the balustrade. She rang the supplier, they quoted, and she placed the order. The doors were to be manufactured in Melle, Germany, with a 12-week lead time.

A friend recommended a builder, who provided an early estimate of cost based on the approved plans. The estimate was a bit more that Marie had anticipated, but she went with it.

The structural engineer went ahead and produced the steelwork detail. The bifolds were heavy, and the glass balustrade was extra thick – it had to be because the beam would be accommodating a very wide single piece of glass, with no intermediary support posts (Marie wanted unblemished vistas of the cityscape, remember). The engineer therefore calculated a chunky 254 mm steel beam to sit under and support this glass weight – not too big, not too small, but exactly the right size to bear the load of all that glass. However, because of its size, the beam could not be fully concealed within the joist; it punched through the ceiling of the bathroom below, creating a bulkhead.

The builder scrutinised the structural plan and saw that he would need to strip off three courses of wall tiles to accommodate the larger beam, and relocate the shower head and extractor fan, before making good the affected walls and ceiling. Unsurprisingly, his estimate jumped up by a few thousand pounds.

The building regulation drawings were finalised and sent off to building control for checking. The inspector noticed the glass balustrade didn't comply with British Standard BS6180 or with building regulation Approved Document K, both of which state that the top of the balustrade must be no less than 1100 mm from the new floor level. The German manufacturer could easily have adjusted the balustrade height had they known of this regulation.

Luckily for Marie, construction hadn't yet started, and the design glitch could be fixed. Had the job started, however, Marie would have needed to order another set of very expensive doors and balustrade, incurring a further 12-week delay in the project plus the cost of the construction downtime on top. The builder could have demanded a king's ransom for the extra work because Marie would have had little practical choice but to accept. And what if the building control inspector hadn't spotted this aberration until after the job was finished? No completion certificate would have been issued until the work was undone and a new, compliant unit fitted in its place.

This process was chaotic, and Marie was understandably vexed, not knowing quite where to direct her grievance. The architect has her defence – she was instructed by the client to design the panoramic windows, and that's what she did. The engineer believes he is in the clear – he crunched the numbers with the information he was given and points the finger at the architect. The builder claims he had a legitimate reason to increase his estimate and sends poor Marie back to the engineer when she questions it. And the German glass manufacturer says they had no way of knowing about the regulatory height and set into production what they were asked to make.

Who *was* to blame in this example?

Each specialist did their job correctly, yet the journey ran about as smoothly as the North Circular past Wembley in rush hour. And this example is no exaggeration. Indeed, it is an oversimplification of what can and does go wrong during extension projects. Regrettably, this sort of fiasco plays out indiscriminately every day in homes across the UK.

The process of extending a home is disjointed from start to end. There is no manual to tell you how it's done, no one authority to govern quality, and no single ombudsman to complain to when it all goes Pete Tong. It is therefore no surprise that many homeowners loathe the experience and fall out with the very team of experts who they entrusted to realise their dream extension. It is also no surprise, then, that the home improvement industry culture is one of arse covering and finger pointing, and of kicking cans down the road.

What is needed is a single source of truth – one place to point fingers at and one place to go for all the answers. But for reasons discussed, that won't come in the form of a person.

**The solution is to have this in the form of a document – one master plan that has been developed iteratively stage by stage, contributed to at the right time by each of the right specialists.**

We call this master plan the *working drawings* (or *working plan*), so named because the drawings actually work by the time they arrive on site. The working drawings are the culmination of all the approved planning drawings, structural detail and building regulations that have already been produced, with the addition of the electrical–mechanical plan and the fixtures/fittings/equipment specifications agreed by the client ... all in one document.

In the event you appoint a specialist supplier to design a specific aspect of the extension (commonly a kitchen or bathroom), their final approved design should be included as an appendix to the working drawings and adhered to by all involved with the same diligence as the rest of the plan.

This maintains the sanctity of the document as the one source of truth for the project.

The working drawings are the Rosetta Stone of the house extension process. A handbook like this, together with the working drawings, are what you need to mitigate against the lack of accountability that comes from an inherently disjointed system.

Next, I suggest a process for you to follow as far as is practical for your house extension. This has been purposefully arranged to ease chafing between specialists and to minimise incongruities between workflows, preventing things from falling through the cracks. Ultimately, this process will help make your home extension a success.

Note: There are various building information modelling (BIM) software solutions on the market, which go a long way towards joining up the fractured process. However, for classic residential home extension-type projects, they are overkill and overpriced, and therefore seldom deployed. As their take-up increases and availability is democratised through end-user friendly apps, one imagines BIMs could become a mainstay in the home improvement marketplace, complementing other guides such as this book.

Let's look now at the second biggest factor leading to project failure.

## 2. Overemphasis on the build phase of the project

> **A common misconception is that the build phase is the project, whereas in fact it forms part of the project.**

As consumers, we are inclined to concentrate purely on the particular purpose – the end result. And we tend to view the *planned work* – everything leading up to it – simply as a means to an end. In fact, the extension project starts the moment you make the definitive decision to extend, and it ends when you finally pay the retention payment to your builder.

However, when the plethora of activities involved in extending a house are untangled and reconstructed into a comprehensible process, the true extent of the project is revealed. Then you will see that there are countless hurdles to clear before you get near a position to start the build. Where project stages are skipped or only partially completed, the seeds of problems that will manifest downstream are laid.

Consider the following illustration.

Andy has a lovely three-bed semi in the suburbs. Like many suburban homes, the plot benefits from a pleasant, south-facing rear garden. Andy's heard that under permitted development, he can get a sizeable six-metre kitchen extension, and what's more, he can start building straight away. This is all he needs to hear to make his mind up – baby number two is on the way, and the kitchen just isn't big enough for all the baby accoutrements and the inevitable pile-up of Calpol syringes.

Andy's sister recently extended her kitchen. The builder did a decent job at her place, and he is free to start pretty much straight away. Andy's neighbour is a quiet, slightly older lady, who keeps to herself and appears indifferent when Andy tells her in passing that the builders will be rocking up to start work on Monday.

After fitting a temporary kitchen (small section of worktop, sink, microwave and mini fridge-freezer) in the living room, the builders start stripping out the back of the house. They make rapid progress, and Andy gets an amazing deal on an ex-display kitchen from the showroom in town.

When the neighbour sees that Andy's extension will sit right on the boundary line, in place of her wisteria-laden trellis fence, she rings her solicitor, who is able to win a near-immediate county court injunction order for breaches of the 1996 Party Wall etc Act. The building work is stopped in its tracks. 11 weeks' worth of microwave meals later, the two neighbours agree on a settlement. Work resumes, and the kitchen extension takes shape.

That is, until the local authority receives an anonymous tip-off that something isn't right. The planning enforcement officer makes an unannounced visit and sees that, although the extension falls within the permitted size allowance, the new kitchen footprint regrettably leaves less than 50% of the original garden intact, which is a material breach of planning rules. The enforcement officer forces the newly built rear elevation to be partially demolished and taken back by one metre.

More time wasted, more money squandered, and a non-refundable ex-display kitchen, which now doesn't fit. To top it all off, the birth of baby number two is now only five weeks away.

As with Marie and her panoramic glass, this type of predicament is commonplace. Andy's home improvement tragedy could easily have been avoided if he had taken the time to do things in the correct sequence, including obtaining the necessary planning and neighbours' consent prior to starting work.

Andy's example highlights how problems not identified upstream of the project can snowball into something ugly and expensive downstream. Let's demystify the project and break the process down into its constituent parts to see how they all need to fit together to make your extension a success.

Note: It is impossible to show the inner workings of every activity within one diagram, so be sure to read the finer details as you progress through the chapters.

# HOW THE IDEAL HOME EXTENSION PROCESS FLOWS

The diagram below gives an overview of the ten stages of any home extension. For a more in-depth view of the steps within each stage, visit www.architecture100.com/book to download our free flowchart.

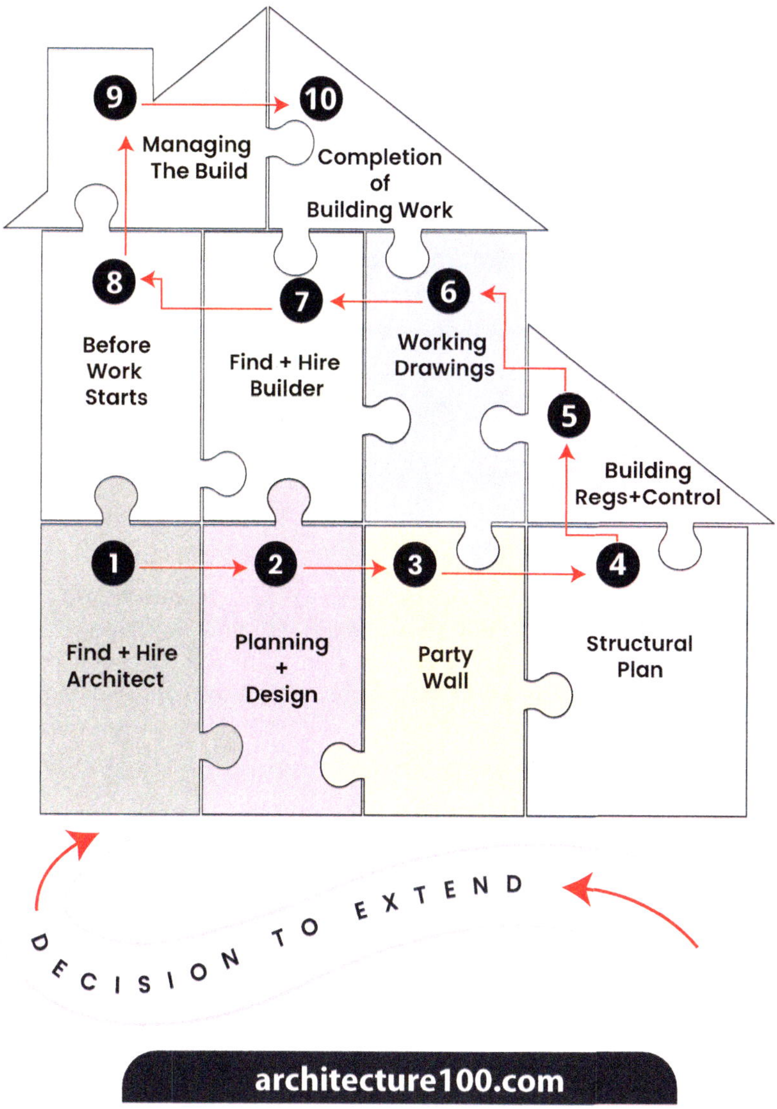

# OVERVIEW OF THE PROJECT STAGES

Before you even start on your project, you will be making the all-important decision on whether you can or need to extend. Extending is expensive and time-consuming, so it's vital to take a number of aspects into consideration before making any significant investment. I therefore like to include the decision making as a process in its own right before the project itself.

After that, I have broken the whole home extension process down into 10 stages, each of which includes a number of actions and requirements as well as helpful tips. By following this list, you will reduce the risk of omitting important work, lessen the friction between people and activities, and increase the odds of successfully navigating the house extension process.

> **It's important to remember before you start that some actions and stages can (and do) run concurrently. Visit www.architecture100.com/book to download our free flowchart, which gives a clear process overview.**

Whilst the following is a generally sound order of how things will work out, there will inevitably be times where multiple actions happen at the same time. Keep reading ahead and thinking about the next stage so you can stay slightly ahead of the game, avoiding stress from unexpected occurrences.

Here's an overview of the 10 stages that follow your decision to extend, all of which will be fleshed out in the following chapters. This disentanglement of the process allows you to appreciate the project in its entirety, and that each phase of the project (not just the build) will require due care and attention if the end result – your perfect home extension – is to be achieved.

### Making the decision to extend

A process in its own right and arguably the most important! In this first section you'll find lots of pros and cons to consider, alongside viable alternatives to extending.

### Stage 1: Finding and hiring an architect

From why you need an architect through to what to expect in their fee proposal, with practical tips on everything in between.

### Stage 2: Design and planning

Identifying your requirements and producing a workable structure to achieve them, whilst ensuring that you'll also be complying with all the planning rules and requirements.

### Stage 3: Party wall

Your extension project isn't only about you. This stage is essential in avoiding conflict with anyone else, especially your neighbours.

### Stage 4: Structural plans

Now you're clear on what you want to plan, this stage is all about how it's going to happen, assisted by your structural engineer.

### Stage 5: Building regulations and building control

Here I've filtered out just enough from the entangled world of building regs and control to enable you to avoid project failure.

### Stage 6: Working drawings (aka working plan)

The final piece in the jigsaw. Together with your approved plans, structural plan and building regulations plan, your working drawings are crucial in enabling your extension to be built.

### Stage 7: Finding and hiring a builder

Tender processes, shortlisting advice, how to avoid marketing traps and what to look out for in building quotes ... there's more to this than gut instinct or trusting a recommendation.

### Stage 8: Before work starts

By this stage, most people trust the builder will take care of everything. But what about payment schedules, prelims and other preparation you need to look after? This chapter will keep you on top of your game.

### Stage 9: Managing the build

One thing you have to accept is that there will always be things that don't go to plan. Here you'll find out all you need to know about managing the unexpected.

### Stage 10: Completion of building work

Everyone loves a happy ending, and this chapter will help you and your builder enjoy a satisfying end to your extension project.

As in many areas of life, Pareto's law holds true for home extensions – 80% of the success of your project is leveraged by the 20% of purposeful action taken before physical building work starts.

So far I have explained the two key reasons that so many home improvements end badly and, more importantly, given an overview of what you can do to avoid them.

The first main reason is that the system is disjointed, which makes it hard to hold people to account. Although you cannot force individuals to take ownership of issues that fall through the cracks, you can work to seal the cracks in the first place. This is achieved by having one source of truth for the project: a full set of working drawings. There will inevitably be a degree of specification change during the physical build, but fully specified drawings in the working drawings will reduce this issue.

All specification changes (either implemented or only enquired about) should be captured on a change order document. This document then serves as a repository of all deviations off baseline (working drawings), and thus provides traceability.

The second culprit contributing to project failure is the overemphasis on the build phase of the project. However, by following the stages and individual steps of the process as outlined, you stand a better chance of nipping any problems in the bud. And it's important to remember that any process is only as good as the people plugged into it, so it's imperative you recruit the best people possible.

In the following chapters we will look at the process stages and steps in more detail. They are not written as exhaustive accounts of each step, because that would be information overload. Instead, to maximise usability, I will share practical tips on how to overcome some of the common pitfalls you may encounter as you jog through your home extension process.

We'll start with the one that comes before any extension project, which other books overlook, but is possibly the most important factor ...

# MAKING THE DECISION TO EXTEND

The fact you are reading this book indicates that you have already, at least partially, invested in the idea of extending your home. However, making the full commitment is a process in itself. It's also the crucial first step before the extension process, so let's consider some of the main factors that need to feed into your decision making.

## Why are you thinking of extending?

Perhaps you crave more space because the size of your household is growing, due to babies on the way or dependants moving in. The Covid pandemic changed the way many of us use our homes – homeworking and home gyms are here to stay, and these amenities need dedicated space. Perhaps finances now permit you to finally extend your kitchen. Or maybe you've come to the resolution that where you live now will be your home for life, and that it therefore warrants investment in futureproofing.

### The first question to ask yourself: What problem am I trying to solve?

Imagine if the owners of an identical pair of adjoining 1930s semi-detached homes both decide to extend into their lofts. One of these homeowners wants to create a luxury bells-and-whistles master bedroom, whilst his neighbour intends to create another rentable room to supplement her state pension. In designing the space and purchasing materials (and following all the other steps in the home extension process) to serve their dissimilar needs, the two neighbours will end up with two very different lofts.

When you've identified your motivation and what you want to achieve, this will serve as your anchor point when making the numerous design and purchasing decisions further down the line.

## What's your backup plan?

There are various reasons an extension may never materialise, so it's important to consider what you would do if yours didn't work out. You may be refused planning consent; the cost of construction may be prohibitively high; a neighbour may kibosh the scheme; or personal circumstances like births, deaths, marriage, divorce, a career change or a knock to your finances could all stop your plans dead in their tracks.

Therefore, think ahead about a plan B in case plan A doesn't work out. One such option would be to move house, particularly when economic stimuli such as stamp duty holidays or guaranteed deposit schemes are in play. These financial incentives could make a move that was previously out of reach suddenly viable. Similarly, you could achieve more living space by moving further out of town. Alternatively, a 'substitute' for a full extension – like a prefabricated garden room or converting an existing space within the footprint of your home – might give you the additional amenity you need. Additionally, flexibility on the scope of the project (downscaling), the timing (delaying) or the budget (increasing), could all once again make extending a realistic option.

## Is this the right time to extend?

Even the best-planned extensions can become arduous if works interfere with important life events, so it is imperative you pull the trigger only when the timings work for you.

There are many milestones in life that you would do well to plan works around. Chief amongst these are schooling and exams (namely 11+, GCSEs and A levels); the arrival of a baby; or known work commitments, where project deadlines or travel will prohibit you from giving the project the attention it requires.

Think also about the project timing in the longer term. It might make sense to extend now, but would it still be a sound decision five years from now? No one knows what the future may hold, but if you plan on having more children, or it's likely a dependent relative may need to move in, perhaps the pragmatic choice for the longer term might be to bite the bullet and upsize ahead of time.

Additionally, consider the timing in relation to wider external matters. What's happening in the economy – are we in recession? Is the job market healthy? What's the trend in the housing market? Is the construction industry sufficiently staffed with skilled labour for the standard of work you expect?

Finally, let's not forget the Great British weather. Although the timing won't particularly impact the builder's availability, you may feel more comfortable undertaking works during the spring and summer months, when general disruption from having a chunk of your home open to the elements is a little more bearable.

## Are your expectations realistic?

Ask any of the professionals you will encounter in the home extension process – builders, tradesmen, architects and surveyors – and they will all tell you that the most difficult aspect of their job is managing their client's expectations. Often, a homeowner's expectations on what things cost, how long they take and what they involve are (to the homeowner's detriment) painfully misinformed. The best advice on this is to bin any such preconceptions and be willing to start your fact-finding afresh.

You'd be forgiven for wondering just how you can make an informed decision now on whether to extend if you wouldn't be gathering realistic quotes and finding all the contractors you need till much later in the process. The process outlined on page 16 and explained throughout this book is designed to give you perspective on the entirety of the process, but it remains a process guide rather than job-specific detail. If you feel you need more insight now, for example on build costs, you can speak to a builder generally about your intended plans. However, take any cost indications with extreme caution – without specificity, they will not be very accurate.

> **It is imperative that you do not base your decision on what you read online, where the content is most likely to be outdated, biased or simply clickbait.**

The sole purpose of speaking to a builder at your initial decision-making stage is to gain some idea of the financial viability of extending. If the numbers you hear are consistently higher than you could realistically budget for, you'll need to think twice before proceeding any further. Also, remember that the builders you informally speak to now should in no way influence the thoroughness with which you formally shortlist builders later in the process.

When it comes to timescales, for most projects involving a planning application, structural work and party wall notices, you should allow 12–20 weeks to get through the architectural stages and party wall matters. The physical build phase will vary hugely from project to project, but whatever plans you and your new team come up with, always allow an additional 20% to the allotted timeframe. This will help you to avoid undue stress – it's very likely your project won't be completed exactly on schedule, so keep other plans on hold for some time after the planned work time.

Finally, be prepared for disruption. Dispel any notions you harbour about the building work happening in harmony with your day-to-day life. Having a building crew on site daily, with delivery trucks bringing tonnes of material to your front door, will inevitably affect how you live your life. There's no such thing as quiet building work, and dust will find its way through the tiniest gaps. The tradesmen will need to disconnect and reconnect utility services from time to time, and you'll be regularly summoned to the building site to make and confirm decisions.

Go into the build phase knowing that life won't be in any way normal for a few weeks or months. If it is too much to bear, you can always move out for the duration of works, but you must still be available to visit the site on most days.

## What else could you do with the cash?

If you're motivated to get more living space because other options simply aren't feasible, you will extend no matter what. However, if you wish to do so out of choice rather than necessity, then as a closing consideration, think about how else you might be able to use the money to improve your lifestyle. The hottest property trend in 2022 is the UK holiday-home market, and it might well be worth investing in a seaside getaway. Indeed, buy-to-let investments generally remain popular, despite the 2017 introduction of the landlord tax. Or perhaps you could join the urban rich in ditching the city for the country, to enjoy being lord of your very own manor. Pondering the alternatives is always a worthwhile exercise. At the very least, you will come away positively reaffirmed in your decision to extend.

> Many homeowners will never have the need or desire to extend their home; some might undertake an extension project once in a lifetime; and others may do so every time they feel the need for more space.
>
> Whatever the case, extending isn't an easy prospect – it is costly, disruptive and time-consuming. It is therefore imperative that you, as homeowner and paymaster, take time to scrutinise all the considerations above before committing yourself to the work.

# SEVEN THINGS LEASEHOLDERS NEED TO CONSIDER BEFORE EXTENDING

Before we dive into the joys of building, let's summarise some leaseholder-specific issues. If you are a freeholder, skip ahead to the next chapter.

In brief, there are seven things that leaseholders need to consider before building an extension.

## 1. Permitted development rights don't apply

Unfair as it is, flats and maisonettes do not benefit from the same generous permitted development rights as freehold properties enjoy. This means any form of extension – loft, kitchen, garage, etc – will require a full planning application to be prepared and submitted for consideration by the local planning authority.

Furthermore, in most councils, the planning guidelines are set to encourage less generous extension footprints than are afforded via the permitted development route.

It is therefore advisable to initially engage an architect only for the planning approval stage, before going on to further design work. Then, when you are satisfied the approved scheme gives you the space you need, proceed further.

## 2. Acquiring the space

Before getting emotionally involved in the idea of that dream extension, check whether you own the space you intend to build into.

Many leaseholders wrongly presume that garden space and garages are demised to them, or that they have automatic air rights for an upward extension, when in fact the airspace above the roofline belongs to the freeholder.

Check exactly what you own, and if you do not presently own the space in which you propose to build, you will first need to acquire it.

## 3. Restrictive covenants within the lease

As a leaseholder, one of the first things you need to check for are any restrictive covenants prohibiting major alterations to the property.

Flat and maisonette leases will likely have clauses to prevent leaseholders carrying out major works without the freeholder's permission, in which case a licence of alteration would be needed. Indeed, it is increasingly common to see houses built on new estates (say, year 2000 onwards) with restrictions preventing any increase in a property's footprint. These will have been imposed for aesthetic reasons, to preserve the look of the estate, or imposed as a condition when planning approval for the development was granted by the council.

## 4. Licence to alter

It is likely the leaseholder will require the freeholder's express consent to carry out any alterations to their property, as this is commonly a restriction set out in the lease. An application must be made to the freeholder, who will require a full specification of works.

If agreed, the freeholder's solicitor will draw up a licence for alterations and sometimes a deed of variation to the lease, which formally records the changes made to the property as well as to maintenance responsibilities around the property's common parts and service charges. The solicitor will substitute a new plan, which is then chronicled at Land Registry.

The leaseholder will have to pay the freeholder's legal and other costs of drawing up the licence and deed. This can also be a convenient time to extend the term of the lease.

## 5. Insurance implications

The creation of an extension to your flat or maisonette probably won't affect your ground rent or service charge, but it will have implications on the insurance contribution you make towards the upkeep of the building.

Say, for example, you own the garden flat of a converted Victorian terraced house and enjoy a 50% share of freehold, which you share with the flat above. Your insurance contribution would also be around 50%. If you obtain planning to extend four metres into the garden, you should expect your insurance contribution to rise in proportion to the enlarged footprint. Any change to your contribution will be negotiated as part of discussions with fellow building residents and freeholders.

## 6. Upgrading communal areas

As a result of horse-trading between you and the (share of) freeholder(s), you may concede to giving a little TLC to the communal areas in the building, in the form of upgrades.

Upgrades can take many forms. As quid pro quo for placing your scaffold footing in the downstairs flat's garden, for instance, you may offer to replace the shared front door. Or in compensation for blocking the shared drive, you may agree to repaint the communal hallways.

Opportunistic neighbours may try to ride the gravy train and put in for unreasonable work requests, so consider carefully how much you are willing to budget for if the communal areas come into discussion.

## 7. Fire safety

Since the 2017 Grenfell disaster, building control has rightly tightened up on fire-safety requirements. The prevention of spread of fire is of paramount importance in blocks of flats, where a block is two or more flats in a shared building. In fact, in May 2021 the London Plan, which forms part of the core planning criteria for the capital's local authorities, was updated to include a new requirement to submit a fire-safety strategy as part of any planning application. As such, depending on the proposed scheme and design of the building, it is possible that homeowners might be required to complete fire upgrade works inside other properties within the building.

It is advised you involve building control as early in the process as is practicable, so you are aware of your obligations in good time.

> In conclusion: if you own a flat or maisonette and have ambitions to renovate, be aware of these considerations specific to leaseholders before building any extension. They can have a weighty bearing on whether a project is viable.

# STAGE 1: FINDING AND HIRING AN ARCHITECT

## FINDING AND HIRING AN ARCHITECT – IN A NUTSHELL

There are legitimate alternatives to hiring an architect for the planning and design of your extension, but the penalties for getting it wrong are high. It therefore always pays to hire a professional for this.

There are different kinds of residential architect, so it helps to know which type will be best suited to your project.

Having identified the right type, go ahead and create a shortlist of architects to approach. Recommendations and the local authority planning register are excellent places to start.

When hiring, be sure to tick off items from the due diligence checklist. Also, ensure that you are completely comfortable with the content of the architect's fee proposal before you go ahead and sign the contract.

For ease of reference, you can find a dead-easy breakdown of architectural services at www.architecture100.com/packages.

# WHY YOU (PROBABLY) NEED AN ARCHITECT

Let's address one thing from the get-go: using an architect to plan and design your extension is not mandatory. You could try DIY-ing the planning application or use an architectural technologist (we will meet technologists again a little later). However, this book is about setting out the house extension process step by step and doesn't apologise for placing architects as key agents facilitating the journey.

Here's why.

Put simply, the reason for suggesting an architect for your extension is that there is too much that could go wrong in the process for you not to employ one.

An architect's role is to create a suitably formed and functional space for their client, by aligning disconnected disciplines and harmonising divergent priorities to produce an approved, compliant and specified plan that is ready to build from.

**AN ARCHITECT'S ROLE** IS TO CREATE A SUITABLY FORMED AND FUNCTIONAL SPACE BY ALIGNING DISCONNECTED DISCIPLINES AND HARMONISING DIVERGENT PRIORITIES TO PRODUCE AN APPROVED, COMPLIANT AND SPECIFIED PLAN THAT IS READY TO BUILD FROM.

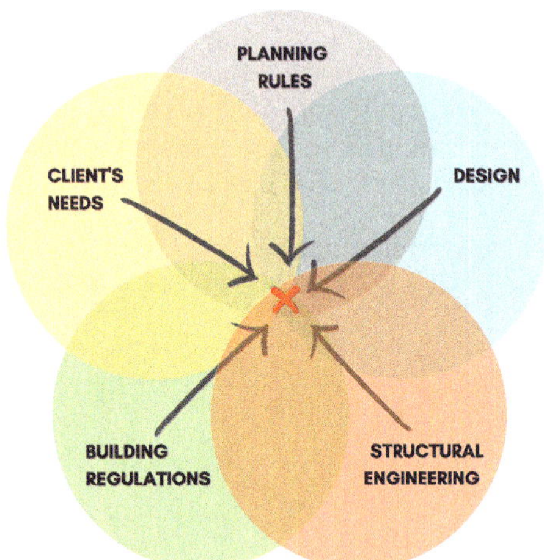


architecture100.com

Let's consider the architect's role in more detail, to appreciate the skills they will bring to your project.

### Creating suitably formed and functional plans

The extension design must be adequately appealing and satisfy the homeowner's practical needs, in equal measure.

### Bringing together disconnected disciplines

An architect will use project plans as a means of connecting the dots between different aspects of the scheme (structural design, aesthetics, regulatory requirements, etc), whilst maintaining overarching administration of the planning and design process.

### Harmonising different priorities

An architect must thread the needle, finding a realistic balance between the (often) conflicting demands of planning, design and engineering.

### Approved and compliant drawings

An architect will be conversant with local planning rules and have real-world knowledge of building regulations, ensuring the project plans satisfy these criteria.

### Plans that are ready to build from

Importantly, an architect will add all the client's specifications to the plans, to a level that leaves no room for doubt in the contractors' mind about exactly what needs to be built.

> Now, that's a lot of expensive plates for a novice to be spinning.
>
> Retaining the services of an architect is therefore strongly advised, to reduce the odds of needing a dustpan and brush for when gravity does its thing.

# ALTERNATIVES TO USING AN ARCHITECT

The title architect is legally protected – it takes seven years of rigorous study in all areas of the architectural field to earn the right to use it. Architects are registered with, and adhere to the code of conduct of, the Architects Registration Board (ARB). We have just read about the main reasons any project would benefit from the services of an architect, but you may still – for one reason or other – prefer not to hire one.

So, what are the alternatives?

## Building without plans

It's true – you can (and some people do) build an extension without plans.

As covered again later, from page 53, permitted development rights afford you the automatic right to extend, so long as you do so to specified guidelines and under specified scenarios. Although these rights technically sidestep the need for planning-level drawings, it is still a minimum requirement to provide the building control inspectorate with structural plans and building regulations drawings, although structural engineers can and normally do provide these.

Only internal renovations that do not alter the building's footprint or remove load-bearing walls might negate the need for any form of drawings whatsoever.

## DIY plans

DIY-ing the plans adds little extra value to not having plans at all, because you are still obliged to produce structural and building regulation drawings for building control.

That said, cloud-based tech has to a degree democratised the design aspect. It is now possible to measure up a property, enter inputs into a design software programme and come up with a visual representation of an extension. This will provide a visualisation of what an extension could look like, and it can help to clarify your own design ideas and give your builder a representation of the finished project you have in mind. (That is, if you haven't already demolished your tablet – some apps can be frightfully frustrating to use.)

However, you must remember that the results cannot be considered to be bona fide design plans, but rather serve as a spacial representation to help give you a sense of the space.

## Design and build companies

Some building firms specialise in one form of extension or other, for example loft extensions, garage conversions or outhouses.

These companies benefit from economies of scale from repetition of design, material selection and construction methods, and the design variables are narrower due to working within a defined space and shape. As a result, they offer to carry out the planning and design function as part of a bundle – a so-called design and build service.

Some design and build companies may have an in-house designer, draftsman and/or technologist, whilst others will farm out the work to independent architectural practices.

These setups can work well, but the repetition of actions can lead to cookie-cut plans. Design and build companies can be hit and miss, so be vigilant if you are considering this route.

## Architectural technologists

The services of an architectural technologist offer another alternative to hiring an architect. An experienced technologist should possess the necessary skills to navigate the planning and design process. Their training is not as intense as that of architects, so some may argue that the barrier to entry is lower. Therefore, is it important to ensure the technologist is registered with the Chartered Institute of Architectural Technologists (CIAT), where members adhere to a code of conduct similar to that of the ARB. And, as with design and build firms, be deliberate in selecting a technologist who knows their stuff.

> Going without, doing it yourself, using an all-in-one company or opting for an architectural technologist are the alternatives to using an architect for your extension.
>
> Some of these solutions are clearly better than others, but the thesis of this book remains the same: if you are planning to undertake a costly home improvement on (probably) the most valuable asset you own, it seems only reasonable to get the very best help available to assist you through the process.

# IDENTIFYING THE RIGHT TYPE OF ARCHITECT

We have established that an architect is a key contributor to the success of your house extension. But with so many types of architects out there, how do you identify which best suits your project?

Types of architect include commercial, industrial, landscape and urban. The best-known type is the residential architect. In residential practice, some architects choose to focus on singular aspects of their trade. It is therefore important to be aware that there are different types of residential architect so that you can identify the ideal one for your project.

## General residential

Generalists have no particular specialism and are comfortable directing the end-to-end planning and design process. This type of architect will read, interpret and apply the local planning policy to your project, to obtain planning consent. They will tether in with the structural engineer on structural design and lay out the applicable building regulations on plan. And they will work with you, the homeowner, to fully specify the details of the scheme on the drawings.

## Planning-focused

Some architects revel in the cut and thrust of planning duels with the local authority and are driven by the thrill of getting plans approved. They will have cultivated productive relationships with planners and have highly developed local knowledge. As such, they opt to focus on this aspect of the process alone, choosing not to get involved in the technical side of things downstream of obtaining planning consent. Amongst other scenarios, planning-focused architects would be suitable where other planning applications in the area have in the past been refused, granted on appeal, or granted with onerous conditions.

## Conservation-focused

Those with a conservation focus will have spent years curating an esoteric, highly specialised knowledge of the ins and outs of getting the green light on schemes proposed in designated conservation areas. Many parts of the country are in planning-controlled conservation areas, designated as such to protect certain aspects of land and property. As such, some architects elect to deploy their specialist know-how to pilot their clients through the conservation minefield.

## Heritage-focused

Historic England (formerly known as English Heritage) have the power to preserve and protect places and buildings of historic importance by 'listing' them. And a heritage-focused architect specialises in working with listed buildings, helping to protect them for future generations. If your property is listed, or a part of it is listed, a local heritage-focused architect would be a good shout.

## Technically focused

The route to a career in professional architecture is well established and challenging. Some spill into the profession from adjacent industries, and it is not uncommon to find architects who double up as structural engineers. Such tend to be more technically minded and have a keen nose for projects that are structurally more complex than the average single-storey kitchen extension. If you're planning on something weird and whacky that might involve a lot of funky structural work, speak to an architect with a strong technical background.

## Compliance-focused

All residential architects will be familiar with building regulations. Perhaps less common are architects who actually enjoy the minutiae of these building codes – there is a lot to get to grips with. It may be that the success of your project rests on someone's ability to know and apply the rules optimally to achieve the space you need. If so, you will want to sniff out a compliance-focused architect.

## Interior-focused

For some architects, designing the interior of a new space represents their creative outlet. Similarly, for homeowners this is where the project truly comes to life. Many architects therefore favour deploying their expertise on interior-led projects, where the skill is to negotiate the line between the possible and the practical.

If you think that you will need to employ an interior designer for your project, it's worth considering if an interior-focused architect could do both jobs.

Note: If an interior designer *is* appointed, get them involved as early as possible and let them lead you on how and when they will dovetail with the planning and design process.

### Sustainability-focused

When it comes to creating a greener built environment, the writing is on the wall – there is a sense of the inevitable in the march towards net zero housing. Mediterranean-style passive cooling, renewable heating and improved insulative building materials are available in the marketplace, and they're now affordable. It is no surprise, then, to learn that an increasing number of architects are upgrading their skill sets to stay ahead of the curve, with many electing to dedicate their careers to designing sustainable homes.

Although all those listed above are residential architects, and all will be technically proficient in taking on an extension-type project, some opt to specialise in a particular aspect of the planning and design process, depending on their experience and area of interest.

When drawing up a shortlist of potential architects for your project, be sure to find out their specialism. That said, on the whole, unless your project demands a specialist skill set, a generalist-type residential architect will be very well suited to the job.

# HOW TO FIND AN ARCHITECT

Having decided on the type of architect you need, the time has come to choose a specific architect for your extension.

> **You should create a shortlist of five architects to speak to at this stage, with a view to receiving three fee proposals – the industry term for quotations.**

Here are six ways to shortlist architects for your project, in descending order of effectiveness.

## Recommendations

This is the first and best place to start your search. Being linked through a mutual contact, your enquiry should carry extra weight, and there is some recourse to the third (referring) party in the event of things not going to plan.

Community groups on Facebook and neighbourhood apps like Nextdoor, WeAlert and OLIO are examples of effective platforms for seeking recommendations. Or you could even go straight to source, knocking on the door of someone who has the kind of extension you want and asking who designed it.

## Planning register

Every council publishes past and present planning applications on their public planning register. Use this database to find applications in your postcode for the type of extension you hope to build. From the search results you will be able to access the submitted drawings, upon which you will find the contact details of the architect.

This is a powerful way to laser-target your search, to shortlist those who have proven themselves to be successful planning agents in your area for your intended type of extension.

## Architect registers

By law, every architect in the UK must be listed on the ARB. The ARB website allows you to search for a specific individual or by geographic area, so this is a sensible place to look. The Royal Institute of British Architects (RIBA) has a similar search facility.

## Trade shows

Here you'll find architects galore, showcasing their services from small exhibition booths. In addition, most home and property exhibitions have an Ask the expert area, where you can drop in and speak free of charge to architects and other professionals about your project. These experts tend to be put forward to the show organisers by their accrediting body, so you know you'll be speaking to very credible professionals.

The drawbacks are that trade shows are generally held annually, and you may need to travel to get to one.

## Social feeds

LinkedIn is a useful place to find architects, where you can read up on their experience and view recent projects they've shouted about. What's more, you can filter by area to find one close to you.

Check out design hubs such as Houzz and Homify. Many architects use these platforms as de facto project portfolios, where you can view previous work and the array of project types they are experienced in.

## Online search

Resort to online searches only if all else fails, because keying in 'find an architect' will return a deluge of marketing directories. These sites are search engine–optimised, and companies pay to appear at the top of search results. A marketing directory acts as middleman between you and the architect and earns a profit from pairing you up.

However, if you tighten up your search term by geographic area or project type, you'll stand a chance of finding a better match. Remember, though, that top billing on search results doesn't automatically mean they are the best. If the positive reviews left by others catch your eye, make a note to follow up on them as part of sense checking when making the hire.

> Use these techniques to create a shortlist of architects you want to talk to.
>
> Before inviting them over, though, call them to prescreen their suitability and availability for your project.

# HIRING AN ARCHITECT

Having created a shortlist of potentials, you are now ready to hire an architect for your extension.

Follow this five-step process to maximise your chances of selecting the architect best suited to your project.

## Step 1: Prepare a preliminary project brief

This should not be confused with a design brief, which we will come to later.

A preliminary project brief should be no more than determining:

- Where and how much space you wish to add to your home
- What you want to do inside that space
- The level of detail you want the plan prepared to

### For example:

*I want to add a single-storey side extension, to give me a dedicated home office off the landing as well as a utility room serving the kitchen. To achieve this, I would like my architect to prepare a full set of plans, all the way through to working drawing level.*

## Step 2: Invite the architect to visit

Most architects will want to come over to see your home before providing you with a fee proposal. Some may already know the area and housing stock well from previous projects and therefore be able to quote you a fee following a desktop study.

Whilst builders can be expected to provide free quotes, it is not uncommon for architects to ask for a nominal fee for their first consultation, which is usually reimbursed upon starting work.

Refrain from idea mining at this stage – the purpose of the visit is to allow the architect to get a clear grasp of the scope and feasibility of the project so they can produce an accurate fee proposal.

## Step 3: Ask questions

Most of the important information you need will hopefully have surfaced as a matter of course through your conversations with your architect. However, to be sure you gain all the information you need, be sure to ask the architect these 12 questions:

1. What do you see as the biggest challenge of the project?
2. What do you consider the most interesting aspect of the project?
3. Are you experienced in working with this local planning authority?
4. Will you manage all communications with the council?
5. If plan A fails, what is plan B?
6. What is your fixed-fee payment structure?
7. Other than your fees, what other associated costs should I budget for in the planning and design process?
8. What are the architectural stages between now and me receiving site-ready plans that I can hand to builders to quote against?
9. What are the best-case and worst-case timelines for the project?
10. Who will be my day-to-day contact, and how can I expect to communicate throughout the process?
11. Do you work with a preferred structural engineer?
12. If there is a problem with the designs when work starts, will you be there to fix it, and will you charge me for that?

## Step 4: Observe due diligence

This needn't be heavy – you just want to be sure everything checks out.

Go onto the ARB listing and confirm the architect's registration (same with RIBA if they're registered there too). Eyeball their portfolio, find a project that interests you and ask the architect about it. Ask for two references from past clients. Most architects will be more than happy to provide these, as it gives them the opportunity to showcase their work.

Finally, satisfy yourself that you enjoy interacting with and can connect with this architect. Yes – that sounds a little abstract, but your gut instinct for a strong working relationship with your architect is sure to yield benefits throughout your project.

## Step 5: Review and accept

In the world of planning and design, residential extension–type projects are relatively straightforward, so you should expect a fixed-fee proposal from your architect.

Their project deliverables should be broken down into (roughly) these stages:

- Planning
- Structural work
- Building regulations
- Technical design

Know exactly what the fixed fee for each stage is, and what peripheral costs you will or could face along the way. We will look a little closer at fee proposals in the next section.

> These are the five simple steps to follow when hiring an architect for your extension.
>
> Step 5 is particularly important, so let's read more into it.

# WHAT TO EXPECT IN AN ARCHITECT'S FEE PROPOSAL

Architects don't have a set quoting template – they will write up a project costing based on their own working system. The different quotes you receive will therefore look different from one another, but so long as they tell you what you need to know, presentation format needn't matter.

The key information you should expect to see in an architect's fee proposal is as follows.

## Overall fee

For residential extensions, insist on a fixed flat fee from the architect, avoiding percentage-based fees or hourly/daily rates. The fee should also state whether VAT is included.

## Stage breakdown

Broadly speaking, you can expect the architectural delivery to be broken down into these four drawing stages:

- Planning
- Structural work
- Building regulations
- Technical design

The proposal should state what the fees are for each stage.

Note: The structural function will likely be outsourced to an associate engineer, and you may be asked to pay them directly.

## Exactly what is in scope

The deliverable is to produce a set of site-ready working drawings. But in addition, you need to know:

- What service level you can expect from the architect
- How you can expect to communicate
- How much, within the fee, you can speak with them about your designs
- How many revision cycles you are entitled to

Quantify what is a reasonable service level for the fee, and what additional servicing would cost. The proposal should also identify other potentials costs ...

## Other costs

The fee proposal should, in some form, list out the other potential outlays you will or could face in association with planning and design. Other costs will be one of four types:

1. **Council fees** – chief of which include planning application fees, pre-application fee and non-material amendment fee
2. **Supplementary architectural fees** – of which the typical examples include the cost of a full measured survey, additional revision cycles, 3D rendering, second application, and pre-application involvement
3. **External professional fees** – in particular those of the structural engineer, and possibly planning consultants and appeals specialists
4. **Survey fees** – for full (non-permitted development) planning applications, the council may ask for additional surveys in support of the application – tree surveys, traffic, topography and drainage, to name a few of the most prevalent ones

## Anticipated timeframes

The nature of planning work doesn't lend itself to predictable schedules, so don't expect precision when diarising interactions downstream, such as those with neighbours, freeholders and builders. However, it is reasonable to expect a best-case and worst-case date range for when an egg might be laid.

## Terms of agreement

The terms of agreement basically form the contract between you and the architect, and you can normally expect these to form a part of the fee proposal itself. This means that by accepting the proposal, you also accept the stated terms of your engagement.

Read the terms of agreement carefully, and query what you don't understand before proceeding.

## Payment method

Finally, the proposal should also make clear the acceptable payment methods, with bank transfer and credit/debit card being the most typical.

This is the information you can expect in an architect's fee proposal.

If any of this information is missing, be sure to ask the question and get the response in writing before making the appointment.

# STAGE 2: DESIGN AND PLANNING

## DESIGN AND PLANNING – IN A NUTSHELL

In residential architecture, the design and planning phase of the project has two functions – unsurprisingly, those of design and planning.

Design is concerned with interpreting the homeowner's requirements and producing a functional, coherent structure that gives them what they need.

Planning is about ensuring the design is observant of the local authority's planning rules and requirements.

The design and planning functions are fused together because the proposed scheme must simultaneously be functionally accurate and compliant with planning protocol.

# SET UP FOR SUCCESS WITH A GOOD DESIGN BRIEF

After taking the decision to extend, the first things you need to do are:

- Produce a good design brief for your architect
- Organise your design ideas in a design journal

These two documents combined are the best way to communicate the deliverables of your home extension to your architect.

One of an architect's most challenging tasks is pinning down the requirements of their clients, who too often have only a fuzzy idea of what they hope to achieve. To ensure you get the most from your interaction with an architect, try to structure your thoughts before contacting them about your design brief. This way, when you do discuss your project, you will do so with clarity and purpose.

A design brief needn't be complicated, although there is a balance to be struck between too little and too much information. Paint a clear picture of what you want, and outline the parameters of the project (the scope), whilst not overloading the brief with too much information to suffocate the architect's design instinct.

> **Set out the destination and let your architect navigate the best route.**

To focus on what's important, try to stick to answering the following questions in your design brief.

- Why do you need more room?
- What type of extension do you need?
- What do you need the new space to do?
- Who will use it, both now and in the future?
- How will the extension change how you use your existing living space?
- Do you envisage any ancillary work, e.g. solar install, bathroom refit, boiler upgrade?
- Where is the line of demarcation, i.e. the physical point that separates that which is in scope from that which is not in scope?
- What are your top three design requirements, in order of priority?
- What type of look do you wish to achieve, e.g. industrial, cosy, period, airy, traditional, minimalist or contemporary?

- Are there any features of your existing home you wish to keep and extenuate?
- Are there any specific (types of) materials, products or brands you wish to use?
- What quality grade do you want to achieve, e.g. top end, basic or average?
- How are you budgeting to achieve that – as much as it takes, the minimum necessary, or somewhere in the middle?
- What timeline are you working towards?

**Your ideas will inevitably evolve, so don't sweat on getting the design brief perfect. It represents an anchor point from which to start, which you come back to as your ideas develop.**

In addition to the brief, start a design journal, which needn't be any more sophisticated than a scrapbook. Here are some tips:

- Ensure the paper is white and unlined – a clear page will help you think freely.
- In your journal, create a mood board for the project.
- Scour through design magazines and take cuttings. Screenshot and print off images you that like from online home design hubs and from social media feeds (Pinterest is a particularly excellent platform for harvesting ideas), and stick them in your journal.
- So you don't miss answers to questions that randomly pop into your head, write them down in the back of the journal to discuss with the architect later – when your reticular activating system kicks in, questions will be hitting you thick and fast.

You can of course find a dozen apps to journal in, but putting pen to paper is always more effective. A physical journal is tactile and will cajole you to discriminate between what you like and don't like, filtering the good from the bad, whilst replacing the fuzzy image of the extension with an increasingly defined one.

To ensure your home extension gets off to a flying start, write a pithy design brief supplemented with a lovingly curated design journal.

These will help put you and your architect on the same wavelength from the start and get your extension plans successfully in motion.

# SET YOUR PRIORITIES

Having decanted your initial thoughts into an edifying design brief and inspiring design journal, you can further organise your project needs by deciding which aspects are most important and must be delivered, and what things you'd be willing to compromise on if necessary.

Start with a brain dump of all the things you want the extension to do and to have, on a single list and in no particular order. Then split the list into three buckets:

1. The things your project **must** have
2. The things your project **should** have
3. The things your project **could** have

When you get thinking about all the various pieces of work involved, you will see how one thing naturally rolls onto another, and before you know it, you've categorically concluded that tearing down the house and building anew is the only way to go.

Take the Khan household, for example:

> Mum has long wanted a kitchen extension large enough to accommodate a family dining table, as well as a separate utility room to store the dog's accoutrements. In addition, Mum doesn't think much of the Artex ceilings in the landing – or the living room's floral wallpaper, for that matter – so she suggests replastering downstairs since the builders will already be there for the extension.
>
> Dad has always fancied marble flooring, but marble is cold to the touch so underfloor heating would be sensible, and that would need a bigger boiler to power it. He also remembers the electrician, when he came for an emergency call out last year, warning that the fuse board doesn't meet current standards.
>
> Grandad always grumbles about having to climb a flight of stairs to use the loo, so he puts in a request for a WC on the ground floor.
>
> Son, meanwhile, lays down his demands for the garden to be remodelled so he can play football on proper turf with goals at either end.
>
> Finally, let's not forget darling daughter, who has just passed her driving test. She sees sense in installing solar panels hooked up to a charge point in the driveway to power her new electric car.

Thinking through the ins and outs of what your home needs can get overwhelming and can very easily lead to scope creep.

Filtering the deliverables into three buckets of varying priority will empower you to focus your budget and energy on the critical aspects, whilst not losing sight of the nice-to-haves that would further enhance the enjoyment and amenity of the new space.

# SUBMITTING THE CORRECT TYPE OF PLANNING APPLICATION

Not all planning consent are the same, and the application type will vary depending on the type of scheme proposed. Although your architect will identify the correct kind of application for your project, it is helpful to know the basics of the different planning pathways.

There are 12 different types associated with residential matters, as follows.

## 1. Householder application

Where permitted development rights are not in play, a householder application will be needed to alter or enlarge a single-dwelling house (not flats or maisonettes, which are treated differently), including for works to other structures within the property boundary. The property should not be listed or sit within a conservation area.

## 2. Outline planning consent

This is not full planning consent but more like getting a decision in principle for a mortgage. You ask the local authority to take a view on whether they would generally support a given proposal before you spend time and money on drawing up detailed plans. Then at a later stage (usually within three years), you follow up with a reserved matters application, which fills out the detail of the proposal.

## 3. Reserved matters

Use this application to flesh out the details of an outline application that has previously been granted. The local authority will typically want to see detail around the development's appearance, scale, layout and access arrangements.

## 4. Full planning application

Again, where permitted development does not apply, this type of consent brings the content of outline and reserved applications together and asks for all the required information to be submitted within one single (full) application. Full consent is always needed for flats and maisonettes, changes of use, or changing the number of dwellings, and for any proposed works outside of the property's garden.

## 5. Listed building consent

If your property is listed or part of your property is listed, you will need this level of consent for alterations.

## 6. Certificate of lawful development

This is an official document, which sanctifies that a development built under permitted development has been done so lawfully. For completeness of paperwork, homeowners should always have a lawful development certificate in their hand when building their extension under permitted development. It will be important for any future insurance claims, for remortgaging or when selling the property.

## 7. Prior approval

Prior approval is conditional approval to develop within the suite of permitted development rights. For residential extensions, this applies to proposals for larger rear extensions (eight metres for a detached house and six metres for other types of houses). The same rules as those permitted development apply but with a twist – your neighbours have 21 days to object to the proposal. If they do not object, consent is granted. If they do object, it's back to the drawing board.

## 8. Removal/variation of conditions

Also known as a section 73 application, this is used for the removal of a restriction and/or condition on an already granted planning permission or listed building consent, such as the use of a particular building material having been restricted. It is also used to seek retrospective consent for works previously carried out without permission.

## 9. Approval (discharge) of conditions

Not to be confused with a section 73 application for the removal of conditions, this is for the approval (discharge) of conditions in circumstances where a condition, in granted planning permission or listed building consent, requires specific details of the application to be approved before works can begin. An example is the final selection of specific building materials.

## 10. Consent under tree preservation orders

If you plan to remove or carry out work on a tree within the catchment of a tree preservation order, you'll need this specific permission to do so. Moreover, if the tree sits in a conservation area and measures at least 75 mm in diameter at 1.5 m from ground level, you will need special consent under the proposed works to trees in conservation areas application.

## 11. Application for non-material amendments

This application is required if you wish to make minor, non-contentious changes to already approved plans, such as the enlargement of a window or door opening.

## 12. Conservation areas

If you live in a conservation area, the type of application required will need extra thought. In the absence of an article 4 direction (more on this later – see page 59), permitted development rights still exist, although they might be curtailed. You could still apply for your extension under permitted development, but the application would need to demonstrate how the proposed scheme would preserve or enhance the aesthetics of the area. If you do live in a conservation area, it is best to engage the local authority early, to get a steer on the most suitable way forward. If the scheme involves demolishing a structure more than $115m^3$, or works to enclosures adjacent to highways more than one metre high, or two metres elsewhere, explicit planning consent for relevant demolition in a conservation area will be required.

These are the 12 types of planning consent pertaining to residential applications, but most commonly, you will likely use one of three:

1. For extension-type projects, a certificate of lawful development is needed to sanctify a permitted development application (with or without prior approval).
2. For extensions that do not meet permitted development criteria, the householder application will likely be necessary.
3. If you own a flat or maisonette, a full planning application will be required.

> You will need to be sure you submit the correct type of planning application, depending on your specific circumstances and scheme type.
>
> Whilst your architect will make this decision for you, it can only help to be aware of the reasons behind their choice.

# PERMITTED DEVELOPMENT

Permitted development rights could allow you to build your extension without explicit planning permission.

Prior to 1995, planning permission for any extension would have been needed. That was until permitted development came into force.

Section 55 of the Town and Country Planning Act 1990 defines development as a building operation (structural alterations, construction, rebuilding, most demolitions); or significant changes of use of land and/or buildings subdivision of a building(s).

Permitted development allows homeowners to extend their homes without seeking full planning permission, provided certain rules around size and styling of the development are adhered to. Works are still subject to building regulations, however, and the rules around what is permitted vary across the UK's different regions.

Here is a rundown of what you are allowed to do under permitted development. The list is an overview and does not cover the technical detail governing what's okay to build and what's not, and not all properties automatically benefit from permitted development rights. As such, it is essential you check with your local authority planning department about what is and is not currently permissible.

- **Porches**
  Keep the porch area below 3 $m^2$, with roof no higher than 3 m and the structure no closer than 2 m from an adjacent highway.
- **Dropped kerbs**
  Dropped kerbs, providing vehicular access from your property to the road, are permissible so long as the road is an unclassified highway.
- **Internal alterations**
  Removal of structural walls is normally allowed but still subject to building regulations.
- **Windows and doors**
  Alterations to and removal or addition of windows and doors to original walls are usually permissible. Bay windows are treated as extensions. Side-facing windows should be of frosted or obscured glass, with no opener less than 1.7 m from the floor.
- **Garage conversions**
  The garage should be integrated within the property footprint, and the conversion must not increase the garage footprint.

- **Single-storey rear extensions**
  Should be built from material similar to that of the original property and not extend past the existing front aspect. The roof cannot exceed 4 m in height or 3 m at the eaves if within 2 m of any boundary. Extension depth must not exceed 4 m for detached properties or 3 m for semi-detached, terraced or end terraced. You can double this allowance if agreed under prior approval.

- **Single-storey side extensions**
  The same conditions apply as for single-storey rear extensions, with the additional rule that side extensions must not be more than half the width of the original property and are not permissible at all under permitted development if the property sits in a conservation area.

- **Conservatories**
  The same conditions apply as for single-storey extensions.

- **Gates, walls and fences**
  Alterations are permissible so long as the property is not listed. Gates and fences should be no more than 2 m high and walls no more than 1 m high if next to a highway.

- **Loft conversions**
  Homeowners can add up to 50 m3 of new space on detached or semi-detached homes and 40 m3 on terraced or end terraced. It is not permissible to raise the roof height or extend past the front roof slope.

- **Rooflights**
  These shouldn't protrude more than 150 mm from the roofline.

- **Double-storey extensions**
  Double-storey extensions must be kept to the rear of the property, be no more than 3 m deep and stay within 7 m of the back-garden wall.

- **Basements**
  These are technically permissible but, following 2008 landmark court rulings, local authorities have become increasingly sensitive to basement developments. Always check with the local authority before commencing any basement plans.

- **Knocking two homes into one**
  This is doable, but check with the local authority first.

  Note: You cannot split one property into two under permitted development.

- **Decking**
  The decked platform should not exceed 30 cm in height, nor should it cover more than 50% of the garden.
- **Swimming pools**
  A swimming pool is fine, so long as it isn't more than 50% of the size of the garden.
- **External wall modifications**
  Maintaining your property (painting, pebble dashing, cladding) is fine, so long as the material is similar to that of the original.
- **Outbuildings**
  These are permissible so long as the outbuilding won't be used as living accommodation. Various conditions govern the roof height, but eaves height must not exceed 2.5 m. Internal size must not exceed 30 $m^2$, and the structure should sit within 2 m of the boundary.
- **Parking spaces**
  Adding parking spaces is allowed, so long as the area is no more than 5 $m^2$ and so long as the ground material used is permeable, or if the driveway design allows for rainwater to run off into a lawn or border, to drain naturally.
- **Change of use to residential**
  It could be possible to convert a commercial, industrial or agricultural site to residential under permitted development. However, the rules governing what you can and cannot do vary depending upon the class of development, and there are a lot of classes. In short, check with the local authority before doing anything.
- **Solar panels**
  These are fine to install, providing the panels don't protrude more than 20 cm from the host wall or roof, and the highest part of the panels sits below the highest point of the existing roof.

The rules around what qualifies for permitted development are updated periodically. What was okay to do then (or at the time this book was written) may not be okay now, and planning permission rules will likely have changed. You will always need to check before doing anything.

Importantly, permitted development rights are not universal, and there are four situations in which they do not apply:

1. Flat or maisonette-type properties
2. Properties in a designated area, including conservation zones, national parks, areas of outstanding natural beauty, world heritage sites, the Norfolk Broads and the Suffolk Broads

3. Areas where an active article 4 direction is in force
4. New-build homes commonly have permitted development rights removed or curtailed at the time planning consent for the development is granted (although sometimes rights are restored after a period of time).

**It is essential to apply for a certificate of lawful development even for permissible work.**

A lawful development certificate is an official document issued by the local authority, proving that the planned development does indeed meet permitted development criteria, giving you peace of mind that the extension is legal. You will need this piece of paper when selling your home, and it is something you should insist on seeing before buying your next home.

Obtaining the certificate from the local authority will take up to eight weeks, but that is fine – you can use this time productively by starting the party wall process (if applicable) and honing your wish list to flesh out a more focused schedule of work.

> To summarise: permitted development rights could allow you to go ahead and build your extension without needing explicit planning consent, so long as certain criteria are met.

# HOW PLANNING APPLICATIONS ARE DECIDED

Large conurbations set and follow a development plan for their area.

Take London, which follows the London Plan – a statutory document written by the Mayor of London's office, setting out the spacial development strategy for Greater London. This feeds into each council's local plan, setting out the area's space and development strategy for the following five years. It sets out the high-level framework for town planning and building design, including for domestic alterations. The policy content is then detailed in a set of supplementary planning documents and guidelines, whose aim is to ensure that a balance is struck between protecting neighbours' interests, retaining quality, maintaining an attractive street scene, and meeting applicants' reasonable expectations for additional living space.

Outside of permitted development, the strength of any planning application is judged on the effectiveness of this balance.

There are five central tenets that a local authority planner will consider when assessing a planning application, as follows.

## 1. Impact on neighbours' amenity

This means that anything in the proposed scheme that impacts your neighbours' current comfort, convenience or pleasure will be assessed. Most notably, this applies to the potential of overshadowing – your neighbours' right to light and their right to privacy.

## 2. Quality of design

The existing aesthetic of a building and/or area should be maintained or enhanced by proposed works. A quality design straddles the line between policy and ambition. It should be suitably scaled and well laid out, and endeavour to protect and enhance the attractiveness of the surrounding environment.

## 3. Impact on nature and wildlife

Certain animals, plants and habitats are protected by law. Examples are bats, badgers and species of nesting birds; trees protected under tree preservation orders; and natural heathland. If any of the above are known to be present in your area, specialist surveys to assess the proposed scheme's impact may be needed.

## 4. Environmental impact

Proposed works that may cause adverse noise, dust, smell or other environmental disturbance could be subject to an environmental impact assessment.

## 5. Other factors

A broad mix of other factors also impact the success of a planning application. In brief, these are:

- Impact on roads and highways
- Parking and access
- Rights of way
- Listed building
- Designated areas
- Flood risk
- Sustainability
- Disabled access
- Sewer adoption and connection
- Archaeological sites
- Restrictive covenants pertaining to conditions of ownership
- Previous decisions made about applications like your own

**Overall, for residential extensions, impact upon neighbours and quality of design are the most significant.**

**Planning policies are not set in stone, but rather living documents that evolve in line with the areas they govern.**

A heap of factors affect planning applications. There is also no sure-fire way to reverse-engineer the success of a planning application, because the context of each individual application will determine how much weight a planner puts on one determining factor over another.

Essentially, it is a judgement call. It is the job of the planner to decide whether a proposed scheme on balance meets the criteria for planning application approval. And it is the job of the architect to make the planner's decision as easy as possible.

# EXTENDING IN ARTICLE 4 AREAS

Under permitted development, homeowners are entitled to carry out certain works (including building an extension) without needing explicit planning consent. This is because said works are already prior approved by the council, so long as you stick to their planning rules.

However, if an article 4 direction is active in an area, some or all of these permitted development rights have been removed or curtailed. Local authorities can use the power of an article 4 direction in several ways that could directly impact your plans. Within Westminster City Council, for instance, permitted development rights for basement developments have been removed. In Newham council, houses in multiple occupancy (HMOs) are not permitted. Meanwhile, in Hillingdon council, thou shall not extend to the rear by more than four metres ... and so the list goes on.

> **Each local authority has their own article 4 considerations, which must be adhered to.**

An article 4 direction does not automatically mean your extension will be refused, but it does make obtaining planning consent less predictable. It means that, instead of taking the permitted development route for your extension, you would need to ask for explicit consent to do so, with a full-blown planning application.

As such, your application will be subject to the rigours of your local authority's supplementary planning guidelines, the design allowances of which are often less generous than one could expect under permitted development. The designs are also subject to scrutiny on the many other aspects discussed in the previous section.

To illustrate the point: an article 4 direction forbids the building out of roof dormers as part of a loft conversion. However, it permits the insertion of sloping roof windows to facilitate a conversion of the attic space, within the existing roofline of the property, thus creating additional living space within the property's geometry.

> An active article 4 direction does not necessarily prohibit the building of an extension, but it does make the planning process a little more capricious.

# GETTING FREE PLANNING ADVICE

Most local authority planning departments will have a duty planner on shift. The duty planner provides handy, (usually) free advice to homeowners on general, non-specific planning process–related matters.

The service gives homeowners the opportunity to talk informally with a duty planning officer to discuss proposals. Taking along documents such as photos of the existing house, proposed elevations and plans, street images and location maps will help the planning officer get a thumbnail feel for the proposed scheme, thereby enhancing the quality of your interaction.

The advice dispensed will typically be on generic matters. It is useful for providing guidance on the local authority's specific planning policy (policies can differ from council to council) and for getting advice on the planning process itself. Although planning departments have quick-reference guides and infographics setting out the decision-tree matrix they work to, it can still be helpful to have this explained in person.

The duty planning officer should also be able to advise the most suitable planning route for your application and provide advice on what types of schemes qualify for permitted development, and what they would typically expect to see on a permitted development proposal.

You will also get advice on how to complete a planning application and, importantly, the officer can carry out a pre-submission validation check to ensure you've prepared the application fully and correctly.

On the flip side, the duty planning officer is unlikely to offer feedback or opinions on specific planning-related queries or discuss the technicalities of a specific plan. And any feedback offered remains the opinion of the individual planning officer on duty and not the local authority, so don't expect to get any advice in writing.

Do not expect the duty planning officer to sign off on any amendments to an existing application or offer up the kind of insights they reveal in paid-for pre-application consultations. This is also not the correct forum to ask for comment on a current enforcement. Additionally, advice on appeals is case-specific and therefore outside of the duty planner's remit.

**Although the duty planning service won't provide targeted advice around specific planning applications, it can still be a useful way to get general advice on the planning process.**

The free advice you receive probably won't be project-specific or in any way binding. However, a duty planner can still be a useful source of general planning-related information in your area.

# PRE-APPLICATION ADVICE

Not to be confused with the duty planning service, pre-application advice could increase your chances of a successful planning application.

Pre-application advice, or pre-app in planning parlance, is a paid-for function within the planning process that allows homeowners to seek scheme-specific feedback on a proposal from a named planning officer from their local authority before an application is formally submitted.

Requesting a pre-app is straightforward. After filling out an online form on the council's portal, you will be assigned a planning officer who will look over your proposed scheme. Some local authorities will share their thoughts by phone, others in writing. Ideal, though, is when the planning officer is willing to meet you face to face – either at their premises or your home.

> **A pre-app could increase the chances of a successful application.**

Opting for pre-app signals that you are seeking a cooperative approach to working with the planning office. All too often, planning officers receive ill-designed proposals that don't meet the planning criteria. To a professional and qualified planning officer, who has spent years honing their skills, this can come across as lazy, incompetent or just plain arrogant. Whatever the reason, it's not a good way to start a relationship. In seeking out their opinion before penning a formal application, you are acknowledging their subject-matter expertise and engaging their support from the off.

The quality of this service really comes down to the planner you are assigned. Some planners will highlight perceived shortcomings and stop at highlighting potential pitfalls. Others will adopt a more collaborative, solution-seeking approach, suggesting edits to the proposal they believe to be more in line with what the council would support. They thereby position themselves better in support of the scheme with every piece of advice offered, because they are letting you know how they'd like to see the proposal presented.

Pre-apps are great at highlighting any immediate red flags. For example, if your property sits in an area known to support a protected species, it could kibosh your extension plans, and your planning officer would rightly advise you not to spend any more time and money on the proposal.

Pre-app meetings, held in your home, carry the benefit of emotive impact. Although the meeting doesn't officially feed into the decision-making process, the applicant's 'natural habitat' showcases the human story behind the drawings, and this can facilitate a more fluid exchange of ideas.

Another welcome side effect of pre-apps is how they open up a direct line of communication between your architect and the planning officer. Whilst emailing over sketches and elevation plans to the assigned officer, you may decide to drop in another cheeky query here or there, such as their preference of window-opening mechanisms, style of lead detailing, or whether a certain type of decorative cladding is acceptable. Every crumb of feedback will help your planning application.

Lastly, pre-apps represent an opportunity to ask the planning officers about any further supporting evidence they would like to see that might support the application. For example, where a proposal includes a glass balustrade, supplying a sample of frosted glass may serve to allay any concerns around privacy.

On the flip side, pre-apps can be expensive, in some parts of the country costing many times more than the application fee itself, and they can add weeks to the decision-making process.

Second, you could end up waiting weeks for feedback that you might get as a matter of course, because there is a feedback loop built into the planning process. If you submit a largely acceptable proposal, but the assigned planning officer sees an obvious improvement that would benefit your planning application, you will normally be allowed a 'free go'. This would allow you to amend and resubmit the proposed plans, according to the feedback provided, without having to start over.

Don't expect any cast-iron guarantees of support, no matter how enthused the planning officer seems. They will use non-committal language when airing their thoughts, awash with words like could, should, may, possibly and likely. It means there is never any feedback you can hold them to if you don't get the result you are hoping for. In fact, this level of repudiation is consecrated in a cheeky get-out clause. Any pre-app advice given remains the sole opinion of the advising officer, not of the local authority, which leaves the door open for planners to change their minds.

This is compounded by the fact that the planning officer assigned for the pre-app may not necessarily be the same officer assigned to assess your full application once it is submitted.

Finally, pre-app advice can have a sting in its tail, namely that it could have a detrimental effect on the proposal if the feedback offered by the advising officer is not acted upon. If you go ahead and do what the planner has suggested you don't do, you will need to provide sound justification for ignoring their advice.

Although it doesn't provide a guarantee of outcome, by any stretch of the imagination, taking pre-application advice from the planning department can be a valuable tool in increasing the chances of success of your planning application.

# FIVE TIPS TO GET PLANNING AND DESIGN OFF TO A FLYER

The start of a new project is an exceptionally exciting – if also daunting – time for homeowners.

Channelling that enthusiasm effectively will help get your design and planning stage off to a successful start, and here are five ways you can do just that.

## 1. Observe etiquette during the architectural survey

It is critical that the measured survey is conducted meticulously. Any errors made here can have material consequences later, so it is imperative the architect (or measuring surveyor, if the task is outsourced) is allowed to go about their task unencumbered. You will quite naturally have questions to ask and thoughts to share, so talk those over with your architect before the start of the survey. If you still haven't had your fill, ask away at the end too, but not whilst the architect is on the job.

## 2. Help yes; hinder no

The local knowledge you hold about the surrounding streets in your immediate area can be of great use to the architect during the planning research stage. For example, you may know the backstory of a particular planning application, and these helpful insights could colour your application for the better. However, be aware not to overload your architect with information – a thesis-worth of your neighbourhood's planning history is likely to hamper progress.

## 3. Don't get caught up on details ... yet

Chiefly, the planning department wants to know what your extension will look like from the outside. Avoid getting caught in the specifics of internal details at this stage – things like light switching arrangements or exactly where the bed will go – because doing so will fetter the progress. There is plenty of opportunity to get under the skin of the plans during the technical design phase (when the working drawings will be prepared).

## 4. Decide the external aspects

During the planning and design phase, it is what happens on the outside that counts, so carefully consider the choice of building material and fenestration for the proposed scheme. This is particularly salient for full and householder-category applications, where any deviations from the approved plan would need to be sanctioned by the planning office, as making changes after consent has been granted may take weeks. However, there is of course a relationship between the siting of windows and doors and the space they serve on the inside, so you will need a decent idea at this point of what the space will be used for.

## 5. Take your time digesting the draft proposal

You will almost certainly feel the urge to ring the architect within moments of eyeballing the plans, to go in with your initial thoughts. Then you'll think some more and go in with another round of feedback. But rather than rushing in, treat the draft proposal as you would a good wine – let it breathe and settle before tasting. Print off the plans and stick them on the wall for a couple of days before deciding what you make of them. This way your contribution will be measured and of greater value to your architect.

> Follow these five tips to help your architect perform their task of designing your extension with minimum fuss, which in turn will make your job of reviewing and okaying the draft proposal that much easier.

# MAKING CHANGES TO APPROVED PLANS

If you followed the advice in the previous section, you will have taken your time to carefully consider the proposed plan before pressing submit. On occasion, however, that thing you were fifty-fifty about gnaws away at you to the point where you feel compelled to go back and change it. Thankfully, there is a mechanism within the planning process that allows for small changes to plans to be made, even after they've been submitted.

The average planning and design cycle, to produce a set of plans that are site-ready, takes 12–20 weeks. In this time your ideas will evolve as the picture of a finished scheme steadily comes clearly into focus.

The planning-level drawings are the first architectural output in the design and planning process. These drawings can be prepared in as little as one week from the time of the measured survey. At the point of submitting the planning application, you will need to have decided what your extension will look like from the outside, and big decisions will need to be made. Choices like the number, size and positions of windows and doors; external materials (such as tile versus brick versus timber cladding); position of walls; and roof type (and more) – all will need locking in.

These are important considerations, which will have meaningful impact on the final form and function of your new space. Some homeowners struggle with this number of decisions in the early stage of the design process, so they end up signing off on plans they are not entirely comfortable with. Planners know this, so the non-material amendment (NMA) mechanism allows for small changes to be made to plans that have already been approved and planning applications that have already been submitted, without needing to scrap them and start afresh.

An NMA request should not fundamentally change the nature of the development, breach planning rules, move walls, increase roof height, or introduce potential overlooking to neighbouring demises. Typical examples of NMA requests include adding additional windows, widening door openings, changing balustrade styling, and other such 'tweaks' to the scheme.

> **Making an NMA is pretty straightforward. You need to show clearly and plainly what it is you want to change on the plan and submit this on a standard application form.**

The fee for submitting an NMA is set by the local authority, but it should be minimal for a standard householder application.

Whether you have purchased a property with existing extension drawings that don't quite work for you, or have changed your mind about something after submitting your own scheme, don't worry.

It is relatively uncomplicated to make small changes to the plan. That said, although this convenient mechanism to deal with minor scheme changes exists, it is always preferable to board a train whilst stationary rather than chase after it once it has departed ... and to get your proposed plans right first time.

# WHAT TO DO IF PLANNING IS REFUSED

You may have produced a great design that ticks all the planning boxes but still find that your proposed scheme is rejected.

If your planning application is refused, you have four options, as follows.

## 1. Resubmit a tweaked plan under the free go mechanism

A free go is where the planning office allow an application to be resubmitted with their advised (usually minor) changes, either upon issuing a refusal or just before they issue a refusal.

The idea is that, where a proposed scheme gets close to something that the council can support, homeowners are given the chance to make alterations in accordance with planners' feedback and do so without incurring additional fees or time.

Generally speaking, if the planners' suggestions are implemented, permission will probably be granted.

## 2. Submit an alternative proposal

This second option is for cases when the initial proposal falls beyond the bounds of practicable adjustments under a free go.

Any alternative scheme will be treated as a new application. It should be sufficiently different from the original; comply with planning guidelines; and, critically, act upon the feedback cited in the refusal letter. For example, if a hip-to-gable loft conversion was deemed overburdensome to the street scene, submitting an alternative proposal with only a rear dormer may be acceptable.

## 3. Formally appeal the refusal

If you cannot stomach the idea of compromising on your dream extension with tweaks and alternatives, your third option is to submit a formal appeal.

The local authority will cite specific reasons for refusing your planning application. If you feel the application was strong, meeting all requisite criteria, and that the grounds of refusal were unmerited, you may have a case to appeal the decision.

You would make your appeal to the Planning Inspectorate – an independent body who will impartially reassess the original application as well as the grounds of refusal and decide whether to overturn or uphold the refusal. Going by experience, and the Planning Portal's own data, you stand a one-in-three chance of having the refusal overturned.

Although you could appeal yourself, it is advised you use a specialist appeals consultant who understands the idiosyncrasies of your specific planning authority.

## 4. Do nothing and simply accept the decision

There are situations in which mounting a challenge would be folly, and no amount of design calisthenics could shift the needle from red to green. For example, if your property is listed or is home to a protected wildlife species, you are very unlikely to overturn the decision. Likewise, if the local authority has an article 4 direction in play, or their planning policy is clearly contrary to what you want to achieve, the writing is on the wall.

> If your planning application is initially refused, you do have options for your next move.
>
> Finding the best option is dependent upon the terms of refusal and on your determination to get what you want (or at least some form of it).

# STAGE 3: PARTY WALL

## PARTY WALL – IN A NUTSHELL

A party wall is the physical wall that divides two adjoining properties.

The centre line of the wall is (typically) halfway through the wall.

In the case of flats and maisonettes, the ceiling/floor separating the two properties is known as a party structure.

Party walls and party structures are likely to be affected when you come to extend your home, and when they are, the 1996 Party Wall etc Act is the piece of legislation that administers the interaction between you and the adjoining owner(s). The act sets out a process for homeowners, which is designed to protect the interests of the people and properties affected by planned works.

Where works are deemed notifiable under the act, party wall matters must be cleared as a prerequisite to starting building work.

# DO I NEED TO TELL THE NEIGHBOURS?

Now that you have settled on a proposed scheme with your architect, it is time to determine whether neighbours need to be informed. If they do, you have a legal duty to notify them about what you are planning to do.

The particulars of party wall matters do get technical, but here is a simplified rundown of the circumstances in which notifying the neighbours will be necessary.

1. Inserting a damp-proof course, even if you are only doing so to your side of the wall
2. Cutting into the neighbouring wall to weatherproof compromised joints and junctions
3. Increasing the thickness of a party wall (where doing so is deemed to have a material impact on the neighbouring side)
4. Taking down and rebuilding a party wall
5. Underpinning the whole or a section of the party wall
6. Undertaking works that necessitate cutting into the party wall for the installation of structural members
7. Building a new storey above the boundary line
8. Constructing a new wall on the boundary line between you and the neighbour(s)
9. Digging foundations (or excavations, as they are referred to in the party wall world), if those excavations (a) lie within three metres of a neighbouring property and will go deeper than said neighbouring foundations; or (b) are within six metres of a neighbouring building, where a line can be drawn at a 45-degree angle between the bottom of your foundation to that of the neighbours.

Minor work involving the party wall – such as rewiring, chasing channels for utilities, plastering, decorating or hanging pictures – is considered de minimis and does not require notification.

If your extension ticks any of the notifiable criteria listed above, you have a legal obligation to tell the neighbour(s) about planned works. The technical term for this is serving notice.

> Essentially, if you want to make your home bigger and are attached to (or in close proximity to) another property, you will almost certainly need to notify your neighbour(s) about your extension.

# SIMPLIFIED GUIDE TO THE PARTY WALL PROCESS

Ask 10 surveyors to explain the party wall process in simple terms, and you will get 20 different answers. (Seriously – try it.) It is not that the surveyors are being difficult; it is because party wall matters are naturally knotty affairs and can quite easily get quite entangled. For now, here is a simplified guide to the party wall process, for your house extension needs.

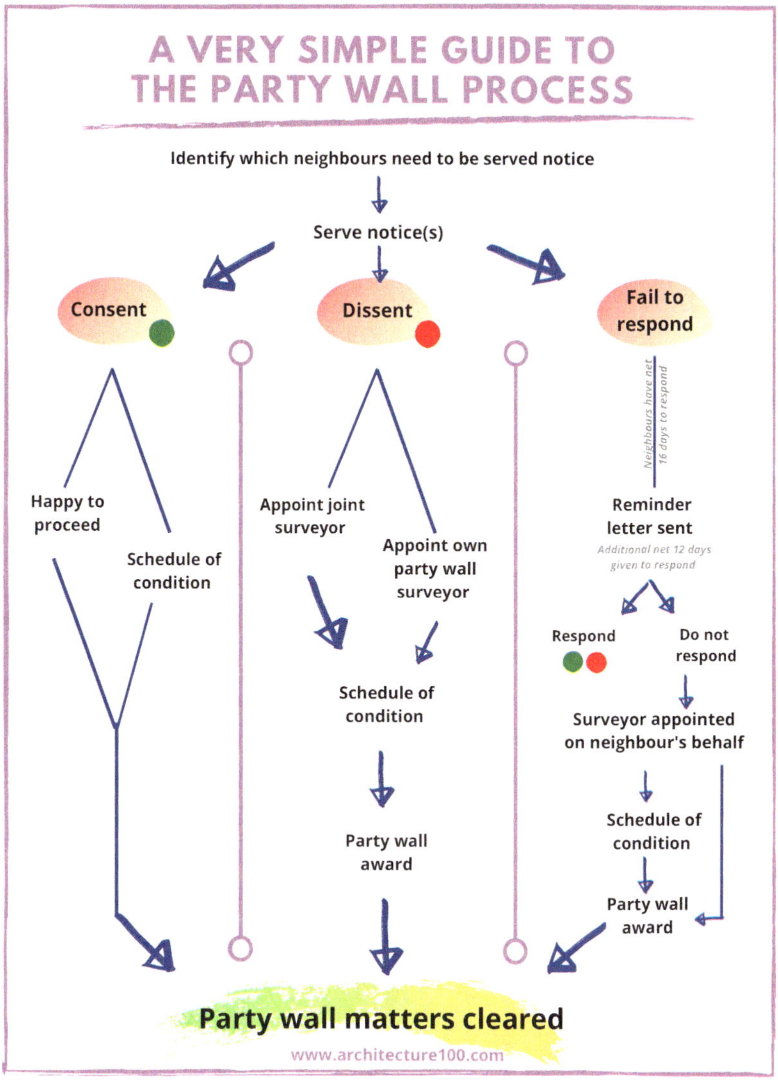

## Identify who is notifiable

First things first – you need to identify which neighbours are notifiable.

If you are in a semi-detached house, it's simply the chap next door. If you are a leaseholder of a top flat in a four-storey block held on a separate freeholding, you will have several notices to serve.

## Serve notice

Once you know who's who, go ahead and serve notice, alongside a copy of your plans.

The neighbour will respond in one of three ways:

1. Consent (agree)
2. Dissent (disagree)
3. Fail to respond

### If they consent

If they are happy for you to proceed, you can go ahead and start building. However, it is strongly advised that you undertake an independent schedule of condition report on the adjoining property, regardless of whether the neighbour asks for one or not. Doing so will protect you against malicious claims of damage.

### If they dissent

If the neighbour is not happy for you to proceed, one of two things will happen. They will either (a) agree to appoint a joint party wall surveyor to act for you both, or (b) appoint their own party wall surveyor to act solely on their behalf. In either instance, a schedule of condition report will be produced (assuming access is granted) and, importantly, a party wall award will be written. This legal document will detail the nature of works to be carried out in relation to party wall matters between you and the neighbour.

### If they fail to respond

If your neighbour fails to respond to the party wall notice after net 16 days, they will get a reminder (called a section 10(4) notice). With a section 10(4) comes a further net 12 days for them to reply. If they still have not responded at this stage, they are deemed to be in dissent, and a party wall surveyor is mandatorily appointed on their behalf. If access to the property is granted, the surveyor will complete a schedule of condition. If access is not granted, a party wall award will be produced anyway. Be aware that even if your neighbour fails to respond to the party wall notice, they cannot stop you from building your extension, but it will lead to a delay.

## Commence building work

If the neighbour consents, you may start work.

If the neighbour dissents or fails to respond, you will eventually be at liberty to start work, upon production of a party wall award.

> Your interactions with neighbours might twist and turn for better or worse, depending on your particular circumstances. However – presuming plans have been approved for the local authority – neighbours cannot prevent you from building your extension; they'll only delay you.

# THE RISKS OF NOT ISSUING NOTICES

If the type of extension you are soon to build is deemed notifiable under the 1996 Party Wall etc Act, you are obliged to serve notice to the relevant neighbours. Not doing so carries expensive, stressful risk.

The dangers of not serving notice to neighbours are five-fold.

## 1. Damage claims

Following the party wall process correctly will protect you from unscrupulous neighbours making malicious claims as a result of building work.

A schedule of condition is an independently written report produced by a party wall surveyor, documenting the state of repair of the adjoining owners' property. It serves as a baseline against which an observer can make before and after inspections of the condition of a property. Thus, any damage caused in the adjoining home as a result of building work can be measured. Without that baseline, you are exposed to the potential of fraudulent claims of damage made by a neighbour.

For instance, your neighbour may have endured a leaky roof for months prior to you commencing building work. If you have failed to serve notice and produce a schedule of condition, your neighbour could then claim the leak was caused by your building work. At this stage, it is your word against theirs, and your neighbours could end up getting their leak fixed with your money.

## 2. Exaggerated damage claims

Not serving party wall notice leaves you open to wickedly exaggerated claims of damage.

Say the scaffolders are hoisting up the scaffolding rig over your house and accidentally drop a fixing bracket, breaking three tiles on the neighbour's kitchen roof below. By the time your neighbour has whipped on his dressing gown and marched over to your front door, the three broken tiles have magically transmuted into 30 shattered tiles across multiple areas of the roof; a smashed-up ceiling; and a wrecked lighting circuit, which has somehow caused the boiler to pack in and inexplicably burn an iron-shaped hole on his bedroom carpet.

Without a baseline schedule of condition, it is on you to prove you are not responsible, and under common law (beyond the confines of the 1996 Party Wall etc Act), you are obliged to put right any damage caused.

## 3. Leaving you exposed

Failure to serve notice puts you on the back foot with a neighbour in the know. If you fail to serve a party wall notice when it is due, your neighbour will have earned the right to question other aspects of your project, such as the quality of tradesmen on the job, the location of the skip on the road, the noise nuisance caused by constant drilling, and the dust kicked up by demolition.

Don't give your neighbour the opportunity to stick their beak into your affairs – it will only wind you up and slow work down.

## 4. Animosity

By not serving party wall notice, you risk creating bad blood in your relationship with the people around you.

You may currently enjoy a cordial relationship with your neighbours – perhaps they hold a spare key for you, sign for parcel deliveries in your absence and are ever ready to keep an eye on your home whilst you're away. These privileges and others like them can quickly disappear when neighbours feel short-changed by not being consulted in advance on your plans.

## 5. Court action

You risk being taken to court if you do not serve party wall notice to neighbours prior to the commencement of works. Your neighbour is at liberty to appoint a solicitor and take out an injunction to stop your project in its tracks. What's more, you would then have to cover legal fees, and a stoppage in work could be very costly if the builder sought to chase you for loss of income.

In addition to potentially heavy costs, project completion will be delayed; and the beautiful new kitchen, in which you hoped to cook a 10 kg Christmas turkey, now won't now be ready till barbeque season. Further still – and more painful than the time and cost involved in an injunction – is the stress of being dragged through the courts at a time when your patience and resilience are already being tested by the building project in your home. It is not a battle you want on your hands.

You could serve party wall notice yourself. However, given what's at stake, the sensible move would be to appoint a professional party wall surveyor to steer you through party wall matters.

You can find a local surveyor by searching online at the Royal Institute of Chartered Surveyors (RICS) or the Faculty of Party Wall Surveyors (FPWS). Or better still, ask your architect for a recommendation.

# THE BEST TIME TO SERVE PARTY WALL NOTICE

Having established that you will need to serve party wall notice to neighbours sometime in advance of starting the build, the next thing to figure out is the optimal moment to do so.

You will see on my house extension process diagram, which you can download free at www.architecture100.com/book, that there is a very specific point in the process to serve notice.

Avoid serving party wall notice too early. If you approach your neighbours before the proposed plans are finalised, you leave yourself unnecessarily open to interference. Some neighbours will relish the opportunity to dissect every detail of your plans and the opportunity to tell you how they think the extension should be designed. Regrettably, a neighbour's opinion of the size and location of doors and windows is often the thin end of the wedge.

On the flip side, if you serve party wall notice too late, you risk the neighbours finding out about your plans for themselves, which could spell trouble for two reasons:

1. It puts you on the backfoot and swings the power pendulum in their direction. If neighbours feel they have been kept in the dark, they may become wary of your plans and adopt a defensive posture when you finally do serve them notice. If they do, expect party wall proceedings to move more slowly.
2. If the plans are submitted before you notify the neighbours, they will almost certainly receive letters from the ambulance chasers. Sadly, there are many surveyors who scour the planning register each morning on the hunt for new applications. Once identified, they write a persuasively worded letter to all adjoining neighbours, in which they intimate that, unless they are appointed, planned works could lead to very bad things. Should the neighbours take the bait and appoint their own surveyor, you will be forced to pay their surveyor's fees on top of yours. To compound matters still further, there would now be another link in the communication chain between you and the neighbour.

**The best time to serve party wall notice to neighbours is when you have finalised the proposed plan with your architect but, crucially, before the application is submitted.**

By knocking on your neighbour's door ahead of time, with a well-though-out, unoffensive scheme, you signal that you have their best interests at heart. This engenders trust and, subsequently, the neighbours will be more amenable to using one party wall surveyor to act for you both, i.e. a joint surveyor. The appointment of a joint surveyor will save you a stack of cash and speed the whole process up.

As an addendum, there is a bonus lever you could pull to move the needle further in your direction. At about the time you are hiring an architect, mention in passing to the neighbours that you may consider extending sometime in the future. This will cushion the ground for a softer landing when you do come to serve notice.

> Serving notice too early can be detrimental to the project, and serving notice too late can damage relations, your timeline and wallet.
>
> The best time to serve party wall notice to neighbours is upon preparation of the proposed plans and prior to the planning application being submitted.

# WHAT HAPPENS IF NEIGHBOURS REFUSE PARTY WALL NOTICE?

This is one of the most common questions homeowners ask in relation to party wall matters prior to building their extension. It is also an inaccurate one.

> **Your neighbours cannot refuse your party wall notice, but they can dissent or fail to respond to it.**

If they happen to dissent or fail to respond, at least one (in case of a joint) surveyor, or at least two (in the case of separate) surveyors will need to be involved in the process, as will some form of formal paperwork. That paperwork can come in two forms: a schedule of condition or a party wall award, or both.

## Schedule of condition

As we touched on earlier, this is an impartial report that documents the state of repair of a property at a given point in time. Although there is no set format to a schedule of condition, it usually consists of a written report together with supporting photographic evidence. Some reports are videorecorded with commentary.

A schedule of condition is effectively an inventory report, within which the surveyor inspects properties, precisely detailing the condition of what they see. For example, if there's a crack in a neighbour's wall, they will document where the crack starts, where it ends, its width and depth, as well as the state of the surface around it. This baselines the condition of the neighbouring properties prior to the commencement of building work, so that any changes that manifest after completion of work can be truthfully measured.

## Party wall award

This is a legally binding document that sets out how works, agreed between you and the adjoining owner, will be carried out in relation to the party wall. It is drafted by your surveyor and the neighbour's surveyor and, importantly, sets out how any objection triggered by the act of neighbours dissenting or not responding would be overcome.

The award comprises:

- The proposed plans with detail of works to the party structure
- The schedule of condition (if carried out)

- Working hours
- Access arrangements to the adjoining property (for scaffolding, side wall rendering and such)
- Any special conditions as to how works must be executed
- Details of financial protection (insurance, contingency held in escrow)
- The process to tackle any remedial works, should the unfortunate occur

> Even if your neighbours do contend party wall notice, they cannot stop you from building. They can, however, make your project cost more and/or cause the start of works to be delayed.
>
> It is therefore always best to issue notices cordially and at the right time, to reduce friction throughout the process.

# HOW TO KEEP NEIGHBOURS HAPPY DURING BUILDING WORK

What do good neighbours and flushing loos have in common?

You don't appreciate them until they're gone.

This is especially pertinent when it comes to home improvements. Chances are, you won't feel the benefit of having a benign neighbour next door, but you certainly will suffer the pain of having a bad one.

Follow these eight tips to keep your neighbours happy during building work and the party wall process.

## 1. Show them what you are planning to do

People fear what they don't know, and you can assuage your neighbours' anxieties by inviting them over to see your plans. They will see the plans at some stage anyway, so by consulting them first on your own terms, you put yourself ahead of the curve.

Do this at the same time as you serve party wall notice (upon preparation of the application but before submission), and share only what your neighbours need to know.

Oh, and tea helps.

## 2. Set expectations

Setting realistic expectations is perhaps the most powerful lever you can pull in keeping neighbours happy during building work.

Tell them upfront that the work may get a little noisy and dusty for the first few weeks. They already know it will, but the act of proactively consulting them (note, consulting, not telling) propagates goodwill. With luck, they will be a little more tolerant of any minor peccadillos that arise during works.

## 3. Don't say something you are unsure about

Neighbours will have questions. If they ask you something you don't know the answer to, don't try to wing it – saying something inaccurate might bite you on the bottom later.

Instead, speak to the right pro and get back to your neighbours with the correct answer.

## 4. Be considerate to the street

The start of works brings with it a level of disruption, with the arrival of delivery lorries, unfamiliar faces, additional vehicles taking up parking spots, skips and Portaloos, plus the inevitable noise brought about by works, none of which will help you make new friends.

However, you can give a nod to the inconvenience of it all by asking your builder to sheet-wrap any scaffolding, erect hoarding, keep skips covered when not in use, refrain from maxing-out the radio volume, avoid keeping any building material on the public highway, and hose down the pavement at the end of each day. These small things will go a long way to maintaining the quiet on the western front.

## 5. Building up to and onto boundaries

Your extension could well involve building up to or onto another property's boundary line. This will inevitably require access to the neighbour's property to dig foundations, point walls, make good roof tiling, fit fascia boards, and so on.

When this happens, be mindful of the fact you are working within someone else's curtilage. Be courteous and have the builders cordon off the work area with stands and sheeting where possible, to keep the action contained where it needs to be. This will protect the neighbour's privacy and physical property, and help curb their annoyance at having to endure the work.

## 6. Offer up red meat

Some neighbours – you know the type – just like to be contrary. If you have the misfortune of having a neighbour of this ilk, they will take glee in finding ways to antagonise your plans.

The way to deal with this sort of neighbour is to serve up a pound of flesh before they find something to make a fuss about. Give them a win by letting them feel they have forced you into doing something you otherwise wouldn't have done – something that in actual fact doesn't cause any harm to the project.

Any such concession depends on your project and circumstances, but classic examples include offering not to work on Sundays, on bank holidays or past 1 pm on Saturdays (which are quiet times they're entitled to already); and only using hand tools on the party wall to minimise disruption (which is good practice anyway).

## 7. Offer up a carrot

Other neighbours mightn't necessarily be cynical towards your extension plans but may still benefit from a little gentle persuasion to neutralise any lingering doubts they harbour.

There is nothing to stop you performing an act of neighbourly kindness such as paying to clear their gutters, cleaning their windows, or fixing their garden fence upon completion of work. Small actions like this can leverage immense goodwill.

## 8. Nip issues in the bud

Even if you hire the best of builders, things can go off piste. If something happens that will upset your neighbours, make fixing the problem priority number one before the issue escalates.

If the scaffolding throws out the neighbour's satellite signal, get the aerial guy over to reinstate it on the same day. If their daffodils experience the underside of a workman's boot, give them a voucher to the garden centre. And if Storm Watchamacallit blows the contents of the piled-high skip over the fence, roll your sleeves up and get tidying.

From these eight tips, pick and mix the tactics you feel will work best to keep your neighbours happy during building work. Then you will experience a smoother ride through the party wall gauntlet and through the building work itself.

# STAGE 4: STRUCTURAL PLANS

## STRUCTURAL PLANS – IN A NUTSHELL

The approved planning-level drawings show what is to be built.

The structural plan shows how the extension will be built.

The structural work will be carried out by a qualified structural engineer once the proposed plans have been approved by the local authority. The engineer is responsible for making two essential contributions to the overall scheme:

1. The structural calculations
2. The resulting structural plan

# WHAT A STRUCTURAL ENGINEER DOES

What an architect is to form, a structural engineer is to function. There are many types of engineers working in a diverse range of fields, designing everything from tunnels to turbines, bridges to boardrooms. A residential structural engineer works with homes and houses and is usually brought into the project by the architect.

As far as your extension goes, the structural engineer will perform three primary functions, as follows.

## 1. Structural surveys and inspections

A structural survey is a thorough, non-invasive examination of the property, to check that the building is structurally sound. The survey will generally be carried out as a prerequisite to calculating the new extension's structural needs.

Some engineers do not conduct a site survey and instead make working assumptions, upon which they base their calculations (more in the section after this on why this is not best practice).

Structural inspections are different from structural surveys. An inspection can be requested to gather specific information the engineer was unable to obtain during a survey. Structural inspections include an invasive look under floors, behind walls, within ceiling voids and/or beneath the ground, to check for any acute or potential breaches in structural integrity; and they are carried out in specific spots around the property.

## 2. Structural calculations

Structural calculations are the mathematical proofs, crunched by the engineer, which demonstrate how the new space will be opened up and how the extension must be constructed, whilst maintaining the structural integrity* of the existing building.

*In construction, the definition of a structure is an assembly of parts designed to carry and transmit load safely from the roof, through down to the footings. And integrity in this context means that a structure is whole and entire. Therefore, the structural integrity of a building is its ability to perform the load-bearing function for which it was designed, without coming apart or warping.

## 3. Structural design

The structural calculations will burp out the structural detail necessary to construct the extension, namely:

- Type and depth of foundations
- Concrete strength
- Type and sizing of steel beams
- Connection detail
- Support over openings
- Loading onto internal walls
- Type and size of spreader plates
- Joist sizing, spans, distancing
- Trimmer detail
- Fixing detail

The net output of the structural calculations is the production of a structural design.

**The planning-level drawings show what will be built.**

**The structural designs detail how it will be built.**

Either your architect will assimilate the structural work into the approved plans, or the engineer will recreate their own drawings upon which the structural design is shown.

Whichever way, the structural design should be unified with the planning-approved drawings, so that you continue to enjoy the sanity of having just one set of plans to concern yourself with.

> In short, structural engineers carry out structural surveys and inspections as required, produce the calculations, and draw up the resulting structural design.

# WHY YOU NEED A STRUCTURAL SURVEY

It is always beneficial if your structural engineer completes a physical survey of your home before producing the calculations and structural design for the extension. Some engineers don't do this, instead relying on assumptions about the building, which later need to be proved or disproved on site. This carries risk.

There are three reasons why an engineer would make assumptions in lieu of physically surveying a property prior to crunching the numbers.

First off, they may deem the proposed extension scheme to be relatively straightforward and thus not warranting a physical site assessment. A 'straightforward scheme' may be something like a single-storey, three-metre kitchen extension, with a couple of windows, a standard door opening, and zero removal of internal walls.

A second reason would be if there's a strong precedent of similar developments in the immediate area, such as in a row of 20 Victorian terraced houses, in which 10 have already carried out the same extension that you plan to. The engineer might then assume that what works for one extension works for another.

A third reason is if the homeowner wishes to save money by not paying for a physical survey. Some engineers service this client type by adopting the sausage-factory approach of churning out high-volume, quick turnaround calculations for a low fee. They keep costs down by substituting a physical site assessment with working assumptions.

Any assumptions made will be marked on the drawings with the portentous words, 'to be checked on site', or similar. Left unchallenged, these assumptions are carried downstream in the process, and later (sometimes surreptitiously) passed on to the builder.

Some of the classic assumptions pertaining to the structural fabric of a building include those made about:

- Load-bearing capacity of internal walls
- Continuity of walls down through a building (notable for upstairs/downstairs flats)
- Direction and span of floor and ceiling joists
- Foundation depth
- Soil type
- Radial spread of tree root systems

**The design of whole schemes can be based on what is essentially educated guesswork. And the risks of guessing wrongly are high.**

Let's say that, for a loft extension, an internal wall is deemed by the engineer to have load-bearing capacity. The steelwork is shown on plan to bridge from one side of the house to another, with size and span calculated just right, based upon having this intermediate wall to rest upon. The spreader plates supporting the beams are sized according to the thickness of the internal wall, and timber floor joists are sized and spaced accordingly.

All hunky-dory on plan.

Your builders start work but soon discover that the wall in question is only a single-brick partition wall, incapable of taking the weight of the engineer's steel beams.

Problem.

Work must now stop whilst investigatory work is carried out by the engineer to figure out a workaround or devise a new structural design altogether. This extra work will need to be paid for by somebody, i.e. the homeowner, and it will disrupt the project timeline. For the builder, pricing up the extra work from this unplanned departure from the project schedule will take time – time away from fee-earning work – which would potentially manifest in a costly bill for additional work. That's if you are lucky. If you're unlucky, the engineer may conclude that there is no viable workaround to the problem. Or perhaps you'll struggle to get hold of the engineer to put it right at all, because they are busy putting out fires elsewhere.

Sadly, scenarios like this play out all the time. That is why you need a structural survey for your extension prior to the production of structural calculations and structural design. And the structural survey must be based on a physical survey of your home rather than relying on assumptions.

# OPENING-UP WORKS

As covered in the previous section, when it comes to drawing up the structural designs for a house extension, the engineer will sometimes make assumptions about the building before crunching the numbers. Doing so carries risks, and where possible it is preferable to carry out opening-up works to the property to baseline what is currently there, minimise guesswork, and better plan for what needs to be done to create the new space safely.

Opening-up works are usually requested by the engineer (and occasionally by the architect) when structural investigations are required.

Opening-up works involve stripping away precise surface areas to reveal a specific section of the underlying structure that the engineer needs to eyeball before producing a suitable structural design for the extension.

The need for opening-up works for an extension can be triggered for a couple of reasons. The engineer may need confirmation that part of a structure is as they believe it to be. Or it might be that they have spotted something around the building (such as cracks) that gives cause for concern, and so further investigation of the issue is deemed necessary.

There are four types of opening-up works common to extensions:

## 1. Trial pits

These are holes (usually $1m^2$) excavated by hand, abutting the outside wall of a building. They are dug to check the depth and type of foundations that the building sits upon.

## 2. Lifting floorboards

This is done to check one of many things, such as the continuity of suspected load-bearing walls, condition of dwarf walls, joist integrity or water table saturation. Care should be taken to disturb only the smallest area of flooring necessary.

## 3. Boarded attics

Attic spaces are sometimes boarded over. This boarding may need to be removed to assess the extent of any voids behind or on the underside of the boarding, or to check joist direction and sizing. Keyhole cameras allow for disruption to be kept to a minimum.

## 4. Exposing walls and ceilings

Plastered sections of walls and/or ceilings may need to be removed, typically to check for the presence of supporting members like reinforced steel girders. Furthermore, it may be necessary to check for the existence of spreader plates supporting said girders, the integrity of the supporting wall, and the nature and quality of any connections.

When carrying out opening-up works for an extension, it is best practice for the structural engineer to be present alongside the tradesmen so they can instruct with precision on what needs exposing. This allows the engineer to inspect first-hand and not have to rely on photos and, importantly, keeps the engineer accountable for the work they produce. Openings should be kept as small as practicable, and any making good should ideally be completed on the same day, straight after the inspection.

> Carrying out opening-up works for an extension can be a headache, but the benefits of doing so outweigh the inconvenience. They allow the structural engineer to accurately baseline the make-up of the building before producing an optimally designed extension structure.

# SEVEN MISTAKES TO AVOID DURING STRUCTURAL DESIGN

At the outset of design work on a house extension, homeowners are involved in setting out the design brief and in providing feedback on planning-level drawings. Then, towards the end, homeowners find themselves the centre of attention as the working drawings are specified around their requirements. The stuff in the middle, however – the structural (and building regulation) work – isn't the sexiest part of the project.

By this stage of reading, you know what you need to know about the structural phase. But here are seven mistakes you need to avoid during the structural design of your extension, to ensure this phase runs as smoothly as possible.

## 1. Not using the architect's recommended structural engineer

Unlike when choosing an architect or builder, you probably won't need to instigate a beauty parade of structural engineers for your extension – chances are, one will come recommended by the architect.

Architects tend to recommend engineers with whom they have worked successfully in the past. If the engineer performs poorly, the architect suffers, so it's in their interest to recommend the best engineer for the job. By appointing an engineer from the cold, you risk introducing uncertainty to the process – whether the two of them will cooperate, whether they use compatible design software, and whether they will see eye to eye on the design.

Whether or not you opt for the architect's recommendation, the structural engineer should be an accredited member of an industry trade body – either the Institute of Structural Engineers (IStructE) or the Institution of Civil Engineers (ICE). This way you will always have recourse to a governing body if needed.

## 2. Leaving structural assumptions unchecked

Although we've already covered this in depth, avoiding this mistake can save so much aggravation, it's worth a second mention.

If the real-world data needed to number crunch are not available at the time of calculating, the engineer might make assumptions about the building or proposed works. Where this is done, instructions 'to check on site' (or words to this effect) are usually slapped onto the drawings.

Ideally, *nothing* should ever be assumed. But where it is, the assumption must be fact-checked before work starts. If fact-checking isn't done until after work has started, and the structural scheme begins to unravel when it is, you could face big delays and significant costs when these issues are straightened out on the hoof.

## 3. Presuming you don't need a structural engineer

By following the house extension process, which you can download free at www.architecture100.com/book, you can be sure to have ticked all the necessary boxes prior to starting work.

Once work does start, it's a temptation for every homeowner to add more to the build schedule when the tradespeople are already on site. Doing so is okay until you carry out an alteration that is structurally significant without first running it past the engineer (or architect).

Knocking out internal walls is a classic example. The builder may assure you they have the experience to order the right beam for the opening, and they may guess right, but nobody should make any structural alterations without consulting the engineer first. The consequences of guessing wrongly can get very serious.

## 4. Doing extra notifiable work without informing building control

Another mistake is carrying out further structural alterations without informing building control that you have done so.

The usual suspects for these omissions include widening external doorways and removing chimney stacks. Structural alterations like these require building control notification and inspection, to ensure they have been carried out correctly and safely. Again, the consequences of failing to do this can be disastrous.

## 5. Keeping the engineer in a passive role

Often structural engineers will produce the calculations and structural design, collect their cheque and call it a day, reckoning their involvement in the project is over.

This may be okay for smaller extensions, but there is always value in keeping the engineer involved in the run-up to the build. In the event of a major construction issue, the engineer may need to play the starring role in getting the problem sorted. Keep the engineer primed and present in case they need to leap into action at short notice.

## 6. Over-engineering for ease

Where walls are being taken down and spaces opened up in the new extension, structural members (typically steel beams) are needed to support weight and transfer loads down to the footings. The precise sizing of these members is calculated by the engineer.

Sometimes, however, engineers habitually oversize members just to be on the safe side. You may think it's better to be safe rather than sorry, but on a job where every millimetre of space matters, unnecessary oversizing of structural members could mean the difference between your new space being cramped or comfortable to live in.

## 7. Hiding structural drawings away in the calculations

It is the engineer's job to design a structural arrangement that works for the extension, so it is always a pity to see the fruits of this labour nestled away, hidden deep within reams of calculations. There they sit, disembodied from the proposed plan and serving a less useful purpose than if the structural arrangements were overlaid upon the approved plans, where they can be easily read and interpreted across the various plan, elevation and sectional views.

> Avoid making these seven mistakes during the structural design of your extension, and you will find the transition to the next phase of the architectural process – the building regulation plans – considerably easier.

# STAGE 5: BUILDING REGULATIONS AND BUILDING CONTROL

## BUILDING REGULATIONS – IN A NUTSHELL

Building regulations are the set of minimum standards for the design, construction and alteration of virtually every building in the UK.

Building regs most definitely apply to building extensions, forming a critical part of your architectural drawings, which will be adhered to during construction.

The technical detail and real-world application of these regulations are set out in a suite of approved documents, which are periodically updated.

Building regulations are statutory and therefore enforceable.

Building control inspectors do the enforcing.

# DIFFERENCE BETWEEN BUILDING REGULATIONS AND BUILDING CONTROL

Homeowners commonly misunderstand the difference between building regulations and building control. It is important to know the distinction so that you are better informed about the house extension process and able to keep pace with some of the more technical conversations and decisions pertaining to your home extension.

## Building regulations

These are the legally enforceable rules describing the minimum standards to which buildings (including extensions to buildings) must be designed and built, with the objective of keeping occupants safe.

Building regulations cover every conceivable aspect of a build, from excavating foundations all the way up to fitting cowls to chimney pots, and everything else in between. The regulations are scrupulously detailed and leave the readers (typically the architect, engineer and builder) in no doubt as to how a particular activity needs to be precisely executed.

The regulations only set out minimum expected standards, and buildings can be designed and built to exceed these. Without regulations, buildings, homes and extensions would be open to dangerous – possibly deadly – construction practices.

Building regulations act as a first line of defence against slap-dash plans and shoddy workmanship, to provide a base level of quality for the aspects of the build they govern.

The building regulations are organised by activity type and set out in a suite of approved documents, which are freely available for anybody to view online. The regulations are periodically updated to reflect advances in material technology, evolving construction practices, and changing environmental conditions, and in response to real-world events in the built environment.

> **The difference between building regulations and building control: building regulations are the building standards, and building control is the function of enforcing those standards.**

## Building control

It is the job of a building control inspector to assess whether a project complies with building regulations. These inspectors may either be employed directly by the local authority or work privately, but their duties and responsibilities don't vary.

The *control* function will happen both on plan and on site.

**On-plan** compliance with building regulations is checked when the extension drawings are submitted (usually by the architect) to the appointed building control authority. There are different types of plan check, but simply put, the inspector will scrutinise the drawings and structural calculations to ensure the designs adhere to minimum quality and safety standards. If they do not, the architect and/or engineer will be asked to update the plans with the feedback provided by the inspector. If they do comply, initial notice is issued and building works are allowed to proceed.

**On site**, the building control inspector will make periodic visits to the building site and will check that specific aspects of the build – I'll explain which later – have been carried out to the required standard. If they have not, the builder must redo the work to bring it up to scratch. Once all on-site checks have been carried out successfully and the building control inspector is in receipt of any installation paperwork requested, a final completion certificate is issued, and the building work is officially signed off.

To recap:

Building regulations are the set of national minimal standards to which buildings must be designed and built.

Building control is the function by which inspectors actually check that these minimum standards have been implemented.

# BUILDING REGULATIONS SIMPLIFIED: WHAT YOU NEED TO KNOW

We know that building regulations are the minimum standards to which your extension must be built. They govern every aspect of construction, exhaustively detailing how things should be. As a homeowner, you aren't expected to know the ins and outs, but it is handy to be familiar with the main points.

The regulations are enumerated over a suite of approved documents – or parts, as they are known – with each approved document covering a different aspect of construction.

Here is a quick summary of what is covered in which part of building regulations:

### Part A – structure

Requires structures to be designed and built safely and robustly, so as not to compromise the structural integrity of other buildings or structures

### Part B – fire safety

Governs fire risk management, fire prevention, and the protection of people and property from fire

### Part C – site preparation and damp proofing

Controls adequate site preparation, weather-tightness, below-ground drainage, and measures for dealing with land contaminants

### Part D – toxic substances

Particularly manages the risks associated with insulation materials

### Part E – soundproofing

Governs sound insulation in buildings, and sound transference between buildings and dwellings

### Part F – ventilation

Concerns the prevention of condensation, and the standards of ventilation and air quality within buildings

### Part G – sanitation, hot water safety and water efficiency

Outlines the minimum expected standards for washing and sanitation amenities, the provision of hot water, and unvented hot water cylinder standards

### Part H – drainage and waste disposal

Lays down the requirements for drainage and sewage provision for foul, greywater and rainwater

### Part J – heating appliances
Governs any appliance that burns fuel for heat

### Part K – stairs, ramps and guards
Regulates the safety standards for stairways, ramps and ladders, and the measures to mitigate falls and collisions and impact in relation to windows and doors

### Part L – conservation of fuel and power
Control of aspects of energy efficiency across all facets of design and construction of buildings

### Part M – disability access
Sets out measures for the access to and movement within buildings for people with disabilities

### Part N – glazing
Regulates the safe use of glazing on and within buildings (applicable in Wales only)

### Part P – electrical safety
Lays down the requirements for the design, installation, inspection and testing of electrical apparatus

### Part Q – security
Ensures that reasonable measures are taken to prevent break-ins (applicable in England only)

### Part R – infrastructure of high-speed electronic communications
Sets out requirements for the installation of cabling and devices delivering broadband speeds in excess of 30 mbps

### Part 7 – materials and workmanship
Insists on the use of 'proper' building materials in construction and for works to be carried out in a 'workmanlike' manner

> The full suite of approved documents is freely available online for further reading.
>
> It is useful to have a quick summary of regulations to hand so that, when you hear your architect, engineer, building control inspector or builder refer to them, you'll be able to follow the conversation and speak the lingo.

## BUILDING REGULATION DRAWINGS

Let's get this straight first: some people refer to these as plans, others as drawings. To avoid confusion, I'll stick with the term building regulation (or building reg) drawings in this section.

Building regulation drawings take all the wordy regulations that apply to your project and distil them into simple and easy-to-read specifications on your extension plans.

In the house extension process, the building reg drawings are produced after the extension plans have been approved by the authority, and before the working drawings are penned. The building reg drawings will be prepared alongside the structural calculations/plan. It is not uncommon for the structurals and building reg drawings to be combined.

Within the building regulation drawings, you will find a decanted version of all the various regulations that apply to your project, and how those regs will be implemented in practice. The drawings include information such as how and where joists can be cut, how thermal values will be met with insulation, the fall required on drain runs, compliance with mechanical ventilation requirements ... the list is comprehensive. All of this is shown over various plan views, elevations and sections, to make it easier for the builder to pick up and see what piece of information relates to where on the building reg drawings.

The building reg drawings and structural outputs are submitted to the appointed building control inspectorate, and they are used as a baseline document from which building control inspectors commence their engagement. However, the building regulation drawings are not sacrosanct, and the appointed inspector is at liberty to ask for further compliance measures to be implemented on site. The potential variance in what happens between the original building reg drawings and the building site can be minimised by opting for a full building control application rather than for simple building notice.

> **Beware. In a bid to save time and effort, CAD technicians occasionally cut and paste the building regulations from one project straight over to another.**

For example, where the loft extension drawings should be showing steel connection detail, instead one finds the regulation details for poured concrete foundations! This is not how you'd want to begin a relationship with the professional in charge of signing off your project.

> The building regulations plan is where you will find the germane building regulations distilled and applied to your specific house extension, in a readable, usable format for your builder.

Note: The London Plan is a statutory spacial planning document with which architects designing new spaces in Greater London need to comply. In March 2021 the London Assembly adopted the new 2021 London Plan. This revision is the first since Grenfell and contains a new requirement to include a fire-safety statement, in addition to the building regulations. At the time of writing, the practical application of this requirement is still being worked through by local authorities, and it would not be a surprise to see the fire-safety requirements tighten further over time and disseminate across other parts of the country.

# SELECTING THE RIGHT TYPE OF BUILDING CONTROL APPLICATION

Prior to starting work, you will need to appoint a building control inspectorate – either local authority or private practice – to carry out the building control function for your home extension.

There are three different types of building control application, as follows.

## 1. Full plan application

Under a full plan application, you will submit a set of final plans to building control. A named building control inspector will scrutinise the detail of these plans with a fine-tooth comb, checking to see that all relevant building regulations have been satisfactorily adhered to on plan. If they have, an approval notice will be issued, and work may commence. If the plans are incongruent with the regulations, amendments will be suggested and the plans rechecked for compliance upon resubmission.

A full plan application ensures all design and construction aspects are up to standard from the get-go. This has two benefits. First, when you invite builders over to quote, they will have clarity on what to price, in turn giving you greater accuracy. Second, it minimises the risk of 'extra work' being discovered as the build unfolds.

The drawback to a full plan application is the length of time the building control inspector will take to look over the plans and provide feedback, which can be up to eight weeks. This is a long time to wait, especially at the point in the process where you should be finalising specifications in readiness for building quotes.

## 2. Building notice application

The option of a building notice application is there to provide an easy pathway for homeowners to start small and uncomplicated work swiftly and without fuss. Unlike a full plan application – where building control will scrutinise the full plans and check compliance with building regulations – under a building notice application, plans are not pre-assessed.

The advantage of a building notice application is that you can start work quickly – only 48 hours after submission. Applying is very simple because you only need to fill out a simple application form accompanied by a site plan.

The drawback is the introduction of uncertainty to the process. By foregoing a pre-assessment, you rely on the expertise of your architect and builder to design and implement the correct building control measures ... and there are a lot of regulations. Should regulatory upgrades be required during construction, the cost of implementation might be more than if they had been specified on plan from the outset.

## 3. Regularisation application

A regularisation application is distinct from the other two types because it is only ever used retrospectively, i.e. after your extension is already built. This type of application should be seen as an emergency lever for homeowners who have fallen foul of the correct procedures.

Regrettably, there are many inadequately informed homeowners out there who bypassed the design and planning process entirely to get their extension built quickly, and thus did not apply for any form of building control involvement at all.

The triggers for a regularisation application are:

- When homeowners need to sell their home but cannot until building control retrospectively signs off works
- When homeowners realise they may have put their home at risk from potentially dangerous workmanship

It is very likely that regularisation will involve opening-up works, to allow for critical aspects to be inspected by building control.

> Full plans, building notice and regularisation are the different types of building control application.
>
> On the proviso that your architect produces a robust set of building regulation drawings alongside the structurals, the building notice will be an acceptable choice of building control application for your house extension.
>
> If the project is particularly complicated, opt for a full plan application.

# DIFFERENCE BETWEEN LOCAL AUTHORITY AND PRIVATE BUILDING CONTROL

You have two options when it comes to appointing building control:

1. Local authority building control
2. Private building control (also referred to as approved inspectors)

The similarities and differences between these are quite nuanced, and one could reasonably argue the pros and cons one way or the other.

First, both local authority inspectors and private inspectors will be suitably qualified to undertake the role of building control. They will have completed building-related studies to degree level or equivalent, and in many cases will also be accredited with the Royal Institute of Chartered Surveyors (RICS) or the Chartered Institute of Building Engineers (CIBE). In addition, both types of inspector will have accumulated hands-on knowledge during study and work.

Both local authority and private building control will consider the same three types of building control application (full application, building notice and regularisation), meaning you can pick either to carry out the inspections for your extension. They both work in the same way, checking plans prior to works commencing, physically inspecting during works, advising of any necessary changes for compliance, and re-inspecting the job prior to signing the project off.

Furthermore, both are subject to waxing and waning busy periods, which can affect their availability and responsiveness.

The differences between local authority and private building control, however, are many. The first difference is that of cost. Local authority building control departments are non-profit, whereas approved inspectors are privately owned businesses. This usually means that private inspectors are a little more expensive than their local authority counterparts.

This cost premium does come with advantages, however. For one, private inspectors are generally regarded as being more responsive than the local authority. Since the success of private inspectors relies on efficiency of turnaround, it serves their interest to be nimble in their day-to-day movements, and they will often attend site with less than 24 hours' notice. They are incentivised to work hard to preserve their business reputation, because they are only ever as good as their last inspection. Also, their area of coverage is wider than that of a local authority inspector, who is tied to administering a defined geographic area.

There are pros and cons to a builder enjoying a pre-existing relationship with a private inspector. On one side, the relationship of trust between builder and inspector can facilitate flexibility in construction methods to achieve the required standards, as well as a pragmatic approach to problem solving. On the flipside, one must be mindful that flexibility doesn't transmute to light-touch inspecting – the inspector is there to serve your best interests, and not to make their own or the builder's life easier.

A final difference between local authority and private building control is that of personnel. When the local authority is appointed, your job is assigned to the department rather than to an individual, so there's a chance you may not have the same inspector attend every visit. In contrast, when appointing privately, you will have a named individual attend your job from start to finish, which gives them a better handle on the consistency of building work and you some peace of mind in knowing who'll be inspecting the work.

> Overall, the differences between local authority and private building control are of little material consequence to your home extension.
>
> Fundamentally, it is most helpful for you to keep in mind that the inspector is there to serve your interests, by ensuring that works are completed as they need to be. Be sure, therefore, to appoint building control yourself, as a means of reinforcing the arrow of accountability from the inspector to you, rather than from the inspector to the builder.

# WHAT HAPPENS ON A BUILDING CONTROL INSPECTION

We now know that most types of home extension will be subject to building control and that there are different types of building control application. What the inspector specifically checks will depend on the type of extension under construction, but now we will consider the aspects of the build that generally get checked during building control inspections.

## Commencement

The commencement meeting kicks off the build phase of the project. In fact, it may not be a meeting at all – sometimes you'll have a phone call and sometimes only email exchange, whilst some inspectors omit this altogether. Where there is a commencement meeting, you will discuss the implementation plan, which is particularly salient if you did not opt for a full plan application, where potential risks would have been flagged early on.

## Foundations

Ground conditions and excavations are checked for load-bearing suitability prior to being filled. Proximity to trees, drains, excavation depth and width are key considerations.

## Oversite

Oversite in construction pertains to preparatory ground works. Before the floor concrete can be poured, the suitability of the substrate beneath it must first be validated, which includes checking the appropriateness of the hardcore used, as well as the damp proofing and floor insulation.

## Damp proofing

Any damp-proof courses, membranes and methane layers are physically eyeballed for compliance before work on brickwork and/or concreting can progress.

## Drainage

This is to ensure the drains have been properly laid, and considers appropriateness of drainage sizing, material type, fall and line, bed and border material and correct rodding points for maintenance. The drains will also be tested (once installed) as part of this inspection.

## Structural beams and openings

The beam openings, footings, sizing and connections will be carefully examined for physical adequacy and cross-checked against the structural calculations previously supplied. Works will only be allowed to progress to the next inspection milestone once this has been satisfied.

## Roof structure and floor joists

Timberwork for the floors and roofs is inspected for adequacy. Amongst the inspected aspects are timber size and grade, structural member centres, bracing, restraints, strapping and noggins.

## Thermal insulation

At this stage of works, the shell and core will be up and internal partition framework constructed. Before the new surfaces can be covered up, the building control inspector will check to ensure that the adequate level and type of thermal insulation has been fitted.

## Fireproofing

Measures to safeguard against fires are assessed, both in the newly extended area and the rest of the house, to ensure a continuous and safe means of escape for inhabitants. Measures can be wide-ranging, depending on the project, though you can expect glazing, staircase, smoke alarms, suitable use of non-combustible materials, and escape routes to be closely examined.

## Completion

This final inspection verifies that the newly extended dwelling meets the various regulations and is fit for habitation.

> Building control inspections are not designed to regulate the quality of workmanship. Rather, they serve a critical function in ensuring that works proceed sequentially and in line with the minimum regulatory standards.
>
> This general list of what gets checked during building control inspections also serves as a convenient project milestone guide to which scheduled stage payments can be hitched. You'll find more on phase payments in Stage 8.

## THREE TIPS FOR GETTING THE MOST FROM BUILDING CONTROL

Now that you know a completion certificate is an essential piece of paper to sanctify the success of your extension, here are three tips to help you get the most out of the building control.

### 1. Familiarise yourself with the regulations

From the outset of your project, you will hear architects, engineers, builders and suppliers expound the legal requirements of this regulation or the practical restrictions imposed by the other.

There are a lot of regulations. In fact, if they were stacked up and placed on the floor, they would stretch halfway up your shin. You don't need to know them all, though – only the ones that apply to residential construction. You also don't need to know the detail, but – as discussed in Stage 5 – having awareness of what regulation pertains to which sphere of activity will make it easier to keep up with the abbreviations and lingo being thrown about by your team.

### 2. Appoint the building control inspectorate directly

Too often homeowners leave it up to their architect or builder to do this.

It is the job of the building control inspector to ensure that minimum regulatory standards are met in the construction of your extension. The building control inspector is de facto working for you, but when appointed by the builder, inspectors can defer to them and forget this important line of reporting, leaving you out of the communication loop.

You want to be in the loop. Filling out the building control appointment form yourself, with your name and contact details, and with your signature on the bottom of the cheque, reinforces the line of reporting between you and the inspector.

### 3. Be present for the building control inspections

This may mean logging into work an hour later or leaving the office a little early, but being on site for these meetings is important. They are where (potential) issues are surfaced and where you see and hear the progress of the job first-hand.

The inspections are like a Grand Prix pit stop, forcing a momentary pause in a frenetic race, where the team can adjust the front wing or tighten the suspension to ensure the car stays on track. As the homeowner, you are the ultimate decision maker and should be present and informed.

> Implementing these three tips will help you get the most out of building control by being present and aware of issues that may (threaten to) arise, and nipping any problems in the bud.

# STAGE 6: WORKING DRAWINGS

## WORKING DRAWINGS – IN A NUTSHELL

In addition to the planning-level drawings that show what will be built, and the structural and building regulation drawings that show how the extension will be built, we have the working drawings (also referred to as working plan or technical drawings).

The working drawings are where you detail the in-depth design specifications to which the extension is to be built. They can be thought of as the manufacturer's instructions for the extension.

The approved plans, structural plan, building regulations plan and working drawings come together to form your final master plan.

# WHY WORKING DRAWINGS ARE IMPORTANT

They go by many names – working plans, detailed drawings, specification plans, technical designs, engineering drawings. For our purposes, I will refer to them as working drawings. Let's look at what these exactly are and why they are important.

Working drawings form an addition layer of detail over the planning-approved drawing, structural and building regulation drawings. They show the dimensional detailed specifications about every aspect of the build. Done properly, they should read as a how-to manual for the builder on site.

In the coming pages, we dive deeper into the specifics of each area. But in brief, on a good set of working drawings you can expect to see detail on:

- Electrical first and second fixings
- Mechanical first and second fixings
- Joinery and ironmongery
- Fenestration
- Roofing
- Trims
- An assortment of other items, from soundproofing to tiling and flooring to décor

Working drawings are critical to the success of your house extension. They constitute a physical harmonisation between your expectations of how the end product should look and your builder's understanding of what they are expected to produce.

The working drawings will be thrashed out between you and the architect. In this technical design session, your architect will encourage you to decide as much as possible ahead of the physical build. The benefit of putting in the effort now is to reduce the chances of variance later. Where there is variance there is uncertainty, and uncertainty can be costly.

For example, imagine you and your architect deem it prudent to have USB-C ports integrated to all power points in the new study but omit this decision from the working drawings. Now your builder goes ahead and supplies standard power sockets. Swapping them at this stage will require another trip to the electrical merchant and cost time to swap out one unit for the other, so a feature that should have cost £30 per unit is now costing you double. Now imagine that sort of correction playing out on something bigger and dearer than a power socket.

The point of working drawings is to minimise the number of chinks in your armour and minimise the risk of expensive miscommunications between you and your team.

A further benefit of a good set of working drawings is the quality of quotes you receive from prospective builders. When you put in the time to think about the detail, you take out the guesswork and increase the accuracy with which your builder can price the job.

> **The higher the quality of working drawings, the higher the quality of quotes you will receive.**

In turn, this empowers you to budget with greater confidence, as you've reduced the chance of cost creep and scope creep after you lock into a contract with your chosen builder.

> Working drawings contain detailed specifications on all aspects of construction and serve as a de facto instruction manual for your builder to follow.
>
> Good-quality working drawings are the keystone in the bridge linking the theory to the building site.

# MECHANICAL SPECIFICATIONS

In residential construction, mechanical specifications predominantly refer to the plumbing, heating and ventilation provisions that will be made for the extension. On the plans, you should expect to see the technical detail on a number of items. Let's take a look at the main ones.

## 1. Drainage

It's important to think through the drainage and first-fix connection detail between your existing house and the extended area. The location of the underground and overground soil stack run can hugely impact the extension's layout, affecting its footprint and foundation, and the configuration of internal spaces. If the stack gets in the way of what you hope to achieve, either plans will need to be adjusted to accommodate it, or a clever workaround will need to be engineered.

## 2. Heating and hot water

An assessment of the existing heating system should be carried out to baseline the heating and hot water capabilities. If the system lacks sufficient oomph to serve the new space, an upgrade will be needed. This might be a simple boiler upgrade, or something more involved such as a whole new heating and hot water system, which might interfere with your desired internal layout. In addition, the UK government intends to ban the installation of gas-fired boilers in homes by mid-2030, so it is becoming increasingly important to consider the installation of greener systems – such as air and ground source heat pumps – to all types of renovation projects.

## 3. Radiator specifications

Mechanical specifications should account for adequate radiator sizing and positioning. A room's heat load requirement should be calculated and an optimally sized radiator selected to serve that space. Let's bust the myth that radiators or electric heaters need to be positioned under or adjacent to windows to be effective – they actually heat space using circulatory convection. However, radiator positioning should not interfere with the practical use of the space. With underfloor heating, pipes need only to be run under areas of pedestrian traffic, and not under dead areas such as cupboards. And where underfloor heating is specified, the space needed to house the manifold should be accounted for.

## 4. Cooling

Thanks to climate change, British summers topping 35°C are no longer unusual. If air-conditioning systems are to be installed, the working drawings will benefit from showing the location of the internal and external units. Indeed, passive cooling systems native to homes in the tropics are a steadily increasing trend, though beyond the remit of this book.

## 5. Ancillary works

Mechanical specifications should include any ancillary works required to facilitate works. For example, this may include rerouting the incoming water mains or gas supply, either wholly or partially, to realise the desired layout; and machinery upgrades like water softeners, booster pumps or accumulators for mist systems.

> Most of the mechanical specifications on plan can be worked through (at least at a high level) in advance of the build phase of the project.
>
> Where applicable, it is advisable to engage the relevant heating or cooling specialists at this stage in the process. If they then advise you that certain changes are needed before they can install their equipment, you have the opportunity to design these into the plan.

# ELECTRICAL SPECIFICATIONS

Considerately designed electrical specifications will give you the confidence that your power, lighting, audio-visual (AV) and data needs have been satisfied. They also give the builder/electrician an unambiguous to-do list of what you want in your extension.

Let's look at the main electrical specs included in a good set of working drawings.

## 1. The consumer unit

Electrical standards are always evolving. New power and lighting circuits must be RCD-protected. If you have an old-style fuse board, you will probably need to upgrade to a new, compliant consumer unit. In some instances, it may be possible to run a secondary (compliant) unit from the old one, solely serving the new extension. Either way, it is good practice to know this early on so you can plan for it.

## 2. Power

The location of every power socket should be identified on plan. Decide whether the sockets are single or double, USB or standard, white plastic face plates or brushed steel. Deciding isn't as easy as it sounds, as you will be forced to think vicariously about how the new space will be used and lived in. For instance, before deciding how many sockets to supply, you will need to decide which wall the television will go on and where you will sit to watch it.

## 3. Lighting and switching design

The same considerations go for lighting and switching design. Think, for example, about ceiling lights versus spotlights, wall lights versus lamps. Ruminate too about the choice of bulb, such as warm or cool, as this will overlap with your decorative and colour selections. These choices are largely personal and informed by the nature of the new space. Is it intimate or open? For utility or leisure? Decisions on lighting will perhaps be the most emotive of all.

## 4. Data

In the noughties you would have been running telephone cables around the house, but today you need to lay the infrastructure for heavy data usage. The digitisation of all aspects of our homes continues at pace, and your household's data consumption will only increase over time. Consider pulling the highest-grade data cables into the extension – the ones that can handle a gig's worth of zeroes and ones without breaking a sweat. Better still, pull the data cables through conduit pipes, to allow for future upgrades and reduced attenuation.

## 5. Audio-visual tech

Resist the temptation to opt for the biggest and best AV products available on the market. Think instead about what you need – too often we see AV kit that doesn't match the room it serves, like cosy 5 $m^2$ living rooms pimped out with Dolby's heavy artillery, when the TV's built-in speakers would be perfectly fine for acoustics in a room that size. Conventional coaxial and gunshot cables are quickly becoming redundant as more traditionally broadcast content is now streamed.

## 6. Smart home tech

Linked to AV needs, we have the consideration of smart home automation and integration systems, which control AV, heating, lighting, security, curtains and more. Such systems are (at least in their full glory) perhaps overkill for a house extension designed under conventional permitted development rights, but they're nonetheless worthy of mention.

## 7. Fire safety and more

The electrical specifications on plan should also take account of the number, location and make of smoke alarms and heat detectors that will be required in the extension and the rest of the house. If any ancillary power or lighting supplies need to serve fixtures or fittings, these should also be marked onto the working drawings. Examples of such would be PIR light sensors to hallways, lighting to cupboards, and power to heated bathroom mirrors. Finally, if you don't already have an electrical car charge point, put one in – it's only a matter of time before you swap the pump for a plug.

> Well-specified electrical detailing on working drawings will ensure you get all the power, lighting, AV and data exactly how and where you need it, thereby reducing the chance of costly on-site errors.

# JOINERY SPECIFICATIONS

For our purposes, the term joinery refers to woodwork and concomitant activities.

Amongst other technical information, a functional set of working drawings should include the joinery specifications on plan for all the woodwork and associated ironmongery-related choices for your new extension.

Here are some of the joinery decisions you will be making as part of the design process.

## 1. Stairs

A well-crafted flight of stairs comprises many interchangeable parts. This woody ensemble needs to be put together such that the components are congruous with one another and also with the house. You will need to specify your choice of handrail, base rail, newel post and cap, whether the treads and stringers are open or closed, and your choice of materials for all the above – softwood, hardwood, glass or metal.

## 2. Internal doors

Where you have internal doors, specify the detail. You will need to identify the operation mechanism, be it sliding into a wall pocket or a conventional swing-type; and the door style/design as well as its fire rating. Coupled with the door, you have ironmongery selections around hinge colours, handles, escutcheons, locks and latches. This information should be scribed onto the plans so there's no doubt about what you expect to be fitted on site.

## 3. Trims and mouldings

Architraves also need selecting and specifying on plan. They occupy an influential spot as bridge between door and floor, where they connect with yet another item that needs to be decided on: the skirting. Ponder carefully what you decide here – these items serve as continuity threads through a room. The same goes for the cornicing and picture and dado rails – that is, if you opt for any part of this trio – because what you decide to omit from your design is as important as what you incorporate.

## 4. Wood flooring

If you select wood flooring, make provisions to show this on plan. This will allow the fitter to make provisions for expansion spacing underneath the skirting, avoiding the need for scotia beading. Ruminate also on the right wood flooring for your new space – laminate, engineered or hardwood.

### 5. Bespoke features

No matter how ergonomically designed the extension, you may still find yourself with the odd bit of space under the stairs, adjacent to chimney stacks, behind the swing of a door or under the roof eaves. In these nooks, consider some bespoke carpentry to provide bonus storage, seating, shelving or other such comfort.

Note: Fitted kitchens, cupboards and wardrobes should be left out of scope of the drawings. They will most probably be supplied and fitted by external specialists, who will conduct their own design work in-house. The only consideration to your working drawings will be to allow for the supply of utilities and the necessary install space, and to adjust room centres accordingly. (It is especially important to do this for lighting design).

> Once you have thought through the joinery specifications with the architect, the working drawings will start to take shape nicely.

# FENESTRATION SPECIFICATIONS

Fenestration in architecture is concerned with the provision of windows and doors in a building. Of all the technical design features that make up the working drawings, fenestration is the most critical to get right. The threshold between good and bad selections is slippery – proceed with care.

Before we go into the types of fenestration you will likely come across, let's look at four overarching factors that should influence your choices, starting with the most important.

### Function

What do you need the windows and doors to do? For every opening, ask yourself why you need it. Is it to provide light or an access point, to give fresh air or just to look nice?

### Cost

Sometimes aspirations do not match budgets, but before settling for less, explore the alternatives that may give you close to what you want to achieve without overspending. For example, you might have your heart set on creating an industrial look, with wall-to-wall Crittall windows, but the cost is proving prohibitive. By swapping out metal for UPVC and opting for a non-branded manufacturer, you can create the same look for less.

### Style

Style is driven by choice of material, size, quantity and composition of openings. What look and feel do you want to achieve with your extension? There are dozens of architectural styles, and your fenestration choices should be sympathetic to the overall design. You may decide to stay in keeping with the existing property or choose to give the extension a distinct look by opting for something contemporary.

### Congruity

Consider how the fenestration selections will sit within and against the immediate street scene and other nearby houses.

Next let's look at the five fenestration groupings you could encounter for your extension.

Note: The final three are not strictly fenestration, but I mention them here because they will probably be supplied by the same window and door company.

## 1. Windows

As far as residential extensions go, there are three types of windows: conventional windows, sloping roof windows and flat roof windows.

A conventional window refers to a window in the wall. There is an infinite number of conventional window subcategories, but the main ones are casement type (think of classic UPVC), sash type and tilt-and-turn type.

Roof windows sit within the slope of the roof and open either completely outward if top-hung; or half in, half out when on a centre pivot. You will get to know these very well if you extend up into the attic.

Flat roof windows, as the name suggests, sit within flat roofs.

Roof windows come in all shapes and sizes, but typically you will be selecting flat glass, curved glass, plastic domed or lantern type. For all the above, you will be deciding whether they are fixed or openable (if the latter, which parts); manually operated or automatic; single-, double- or triple-glazed; coated or clear; amongst other choices.

## 2. Doors

External doors are a world unto themselves, with an endless choice of materials, sizes, shapes, operation types, colours, finishes, locks, security, thresholds and letter boxes. When selecting, keep in mind the four overarching design considerations previously mentioned.

## 3. Glass balustrades

You will encounter balustrades in one of three scenarios: doing the job of conventional spindles on a flight of stairs, on a balcony (Juliet or traditional), or featuring as the enclosure to a roof terrace. Depending on the size of the space, these pieces of glass can get very big and very heavy. So heavy, in fact, that they may even need structural support of their own, so it is advisable to keep design and cost in the same conversation when deciding. Glazing can be transparent or opaque, and the finish should be congruent with the accompanying accoutrements (the ironmongery handrails and fixings).

## 4. Bespoke features

A bespoke glazed feature is pretty much anything that you cannot pick out and order from a supplier's stocked inventory. You might have designed non-standard windows to span wall-to-wall and floor-to-ceiling, to create a panoramic vista from a new bedroom; or a small triangular window inset to a dormer cheek; or a replication of a historic gothic opening; or perhaps a stained-glass feature. Whatever the intention, when done well, bespoke glazing can be a real focal point in any new space.

## 5. Internal glazing

In place of a traditional internal partition, you could opt for glass. Glass partitions are fantastic for providing the separation of a conventional room, whilst giving the surrounding area a sense of wholeness by unifying the space with light. Very zen. The fire-safety requirements can be onerous and manufacturing lead times long, so know the implications of both in advance of making your decisions. Same goes for borrowed light panels.

> The upshot of pinning down your fenestration specifications on plan is that there are very many ways to plug the openings in the extension walls and roof with doors and windows. It's therefore imperative that you consider your choices from all angles before finalising your decisions.

# OTHER SPECIFICATIONS

On a set of residential working drawings, the key specifications to capture are the electrical–mechanical, joinery and fenestration selections. There are various other details that could also be captured, depending on how much detail you want to go into.

Here is a brief rundown of the key additions that could be scribed onto the working drawings.

Sections of roof extended should already be shown on the working drawings, and where they are, they should show roof tile type. Any further re-roofing should show tile sections and lead detailing, as appropriate. Furthermore, the styles and materials of fascias, soffits and guttering could be shown.

On internal tiling, decide which surfaces are to be tiled and which not. The same goes for flooring – if you opt for a floor covering that requires installation by the builder, such as wood flooring, resin or lino, mark on plan which floors will be covered and with what.

If any soundproofing measures are being implemented, specify precisely on the drawings where and what type.

If the extension benefits from any special features or installations hitherto not mentioned, it is good practice to indicate these on the plans in case their inclusion has knock-on effects on related areas of work. Examples include exposed brick walls; lead, zinc, copper, timber or other such surface cladding; feature walls; solar panels; repointing; and wood burners, amongst others.

> The line between specifying too much detail and too little is easily crossed, but stick with this list of additional details.
>
> Combine them with your electrical–mechanical, joinery and fenestration choices, and your working drawings will be in good shape to hand to a builder to price.

## WORKING WITH EXTERNAL SUPPLIERS

In addition to the technical detail you'll be specifying on plan, your drawings might also need to dovetail with designs from external suppliers. There are six potential suppliers whose technical design will need to be accommodated in the working drawings.

When it comes to kitchens, you will make arrangements in one of two ways:

- Leave it to the builder to measure up the space and supply a kitchen design from their go-to joinery.
- Opt for the design route and head over to a kitchen showroom/ supplier yourself.

With the former, there are no specific inputs to the working drawings, as implementation takes place on site during fitting.

With the latter, you will visit showrooms in advance of the build, armed with your extension plans. In this scenario, the kitchen designer will work with the dimensions you supply to design a bespoke scheme you'll (hopefully) love. Based on this design, your builder will know which points to run utilities to. These runs should be marked on the working drawings, and the kitchen designs should be placed as an addendum to your master plan, for easy reference.

It is largely the same story with bathrooms. The loo takes centre stage when designing a bathroom, as it must be connected to a rigid four-inch stack pipe, and this can have substantial bearing not only on the design of the bathroom, but on the new space as a whole. Because the stack cannot bend or twist or be made smaller, it is the anchor point around which the rest of the bathroom fixtures and fittings must fit. Macerators can provide flexibility and thus additional configuration options. But they come with drawbacks, most notable of which is the introduction of a mechanical point of failure to the drainage system. Features like wall-hung toilets, powered cabinetry, heated mirrors and the depth of the shower tray are a few things that will require pre-work before installation is possible. Wet rooms will require even more preparatory work.

Thankfully, the wardrobe requirement will be less involved, and the only essential detail to capture on plan is where in a room any wardrobes will be located. This is to ensure that the new (reduced) floor space can be recentred for the location of light fittings, that power sockets aren't lost behind units, that cupboard doors can swing open, and that power has been supplied where it's needed for the fitters.

Sometimes, whether or not a hitherto theorised staircase works in practice can come down to the smallest of margins. It is therefore imperative that the staircase manufacturers get early sight of the extension plan, and that your architect makes any necessary adjustments to the scheme in order to accommodate the installation. Like the soil stack, the staircase is a feature that needs billeting, without compromise or deviation, on account of the strict building regulations governing its design.

In the main, save the usual exemptions, air-conditioning units can be installed under permitted development. However, it is not uncommon for councils to ask for the technical details of the proposed unit, to satisfy any noise pollution concerns. An external unit will need to be cited appropriately, and the internal unit will need to be housed somewhere sympathetic to the new space; and both will need to be worked into the drawings.

Finally, in a similar vein, conventional heating firms and green energy companies (solar, ground source heat pumps, etc) will also need to install internal and external units. The size, spacing, utility connections and maintenance access of these should be marked on the drawings. In some cases, preparatory works must be carried out by the builder; or indeed by the structural engineer, if structural openings or reinforcements are needed for install.

There are other suppliers whose work may overlap with the production of your working drawings, but their services are less commonly retained for a classic home extension. These include audio-visual, home automation and green tech installers, interior designers and landscapers.

You may find yourself working with external suppliers who produce their own technical detail. You won't need to import their design to your working drawings, but adequate allowances for the inclusion of externally supplied features should be made.

Importantly, this will give you and your builder foresight of any preparatory works that may be needed.

Externally supplied designs should be addended to the rest of your plans, for ease of reference.

# HOW TO SQUEEZE MORE VALUE FROM WORKING DRAWINGS

Having covered the must-know information on your extension's technical designs, here are four bonus tips to help squeeze even more value out of the working drawings.

## 1. Zoomed-in detail

If a particular part of the extension drawings is deemed mission-critical or warrants a closer look, a zoomed-in, detailed view is a good idea. An example might be the exact size and position of a supporting pillar in a kitchen, where seeing the detail could determine whether a set of bifolding doors is achievable, or if the depth of joist hangers will impede onto ceilings below. In such cases, a zoomed-in detail showing measurements can really help with touch-and-go decisions.

## 2. Size and space information

It goes without saying that plans will be to scale (typically 1:50 or 1:100 for extensions), which allows the builder to measure out with a scale rule the location of starter walls and stud partitions, measure surface areas for buying quantities, and so forth. To make life a little easier, it is also worth showing the room dimensions on plan, which costs nothing to add and will serve as a sense check for the tradesmen on site.

## 3. Inserting furniture and people

If adding room dimensions makes the tradesmen's jobs easier, inserting scaled furniture and people to the drawings will make your life easier. Getting to grips with real-life space sizing can be challenging to perceive, even for experienced eyes, and rooms can look misleadingly larger on a clean, white sheet of A3 paper than they will be in real life. However, dropping a double bed into the plan view of your new bedroom, for example, acts as a yardstick by instantly putting the space into context. Indeed, the same is true when a human figure is placed into the side-on sectional view, allowing you to see the height of a room as it really is.

## 4. Supplemental 3D images

Sometimes, no matter how many room dimensions have been inserted or how many bits of furniture shown, it remains devilishly difficult to get a tangible feel for the new space. That's where 3D imagery can help. 3D rendering software is used to produce an accurate likeness of how the extension will look and feel, giving you an accurate sense of the space you can expect to enjoy by the end. In addition, for quirkier designs, 3D images will help the builder to understand the vision you have for the new space, in just the same way putting a jigsaw together is easier when you have the final picture on the box in front of you. It is worth spending a few extra pounds for 3D imagery; or better still, on a full video render.

> These bonus tips help get the most out of your working drawings by providing another lens through which to appreciate the scheme.
>
> The better you understand the space you have, the better-quality decisions you will make, and the closer the built extension will be to the design.

# STAGE 7: FINDING AND HIRING A BUILDER

## FINDING AND HIRING A BUILDER – IN A NUTSHELL

Finding and hiring the right builder is a process in itself.

Start with a shortlist of five potential builders by asking for trusted recommendations, checking out builders' accreditations and tapping up their social feeds, being careful to swerve the marketing traps.

That done, invite your top three over to quote, and when they do, ask questions and be on the lookout for non-verbal clues to help build up a picture of how the builder operates.

When the quotes are in, make sure they cover the key information (covered below).

After that, when you have one building company in pole position to build your extension, go ahead and carry out the necessary due diligence before signing contracts and hiring.

# PROS AND CONS OF A TENDER PROCESS

Tendering provides a formal way to receive and compare quotes for your building project, but is it necessarily the best approach for your extension? Let's weigh up the pros and cons of a tender process.

## What is a tender?

In construction, a tender (or tender process, as it is also referred to) is where a beauty parade of builders are invited to quote for a job by first inspecting the site, then raising queries, and finally submitting their bid using a pre-prepared quotation template provided to them by you or your architect.

### Pros of a formal tender

1. The tender process will be administered by your architect, so you have the security of a familiar and trusted guide as you engage builders.
2. The formality of the process helps to weed out flaky builders.
3. The set structure of sending invitations, reviewing submissions, interviewing, and accepting bids serves to attract professional builders.
4. A formal tender will include multiple schedules of work for different activities. By writing it all down, you leave nothing to chance.
5. Parcelling up different schedules of work makes it easier and neater to subcontract the work out to different suppliers.
6. Formal tendering provides a set format for builders to quote within, making it easier to compare like with like.

### Cons of a formal tender

1. You can administer the quote-collection process yourself. It isn't difficult, nor should it be daunting – by now you understand the scheme as well as anyone. It also then doesn't cost you anything.
2. The formality of the process is a double-edged sword and leads to self-selection of a certain (pricier) breed of builder. Tender documentation is exhaustive and will take a builder a lot of time, patience and technical research to fully understand. Often, builders will have a quantity surveyor in-house or on retention to price up tenders for work. This overhead will be reflected in their price.
3. On the flipside, tendering may scare off other talented builders who aren't disposed to go through the tender process, because they can win work more easily elsewhere without needing to jump through

hoops. The builder pool is therefore diminished (which is why you tend to see the same old faces winning contract after contract in the public sector).

4. Although writing out various technical schedules means nothing is left to chance, the thoroughness of the schedule is only as good as the person writing it. Too often, tenders are verbose and overly complicated. There is questionable benefit in writing out in words what the drawings already show on plan. If a builder can quote on plan and provide a side list of assumptions made, and considerations and exclusions to scope, that's a very good place to start.
5. Tenders often combine work into different activity types, which is ideal when you have various specialist tradesmen on site, each doing one thing, as on large new-build developments. In the home improvement and renovation sector, builders will have smaller teams with multi-functional tradesmen, who won't have the luxury of just doing one thing. As such, this negates the benefit of delineation.
6. Set quoting formats do provide a framework for consistency, but so do quality working drawings. A well-specified set of working drawings will have the approved plans, structural designs and building regulation requirements, together with all the technical specifications and client selections, all in one place. So the working drawings themselves provide the set format for builders to quote against, allowing you to confidently compare like for like.

After weighing up the pros and cons of a tender process, we see that tenders have their place, being well suited for medium-to-large or complex projects. However, the drawbacks can outweigh the benefits when applied to classic house extensions, where tendering offers no more value than a quality set of working drawings.

# HOW TO SHORTLIST GOOD BUILDERS

We are now approaching the point in the process that a lot of homeowners feel most anxious about: asking builders for quotes. Unfortunately, this anxiety is at least in part well placed, because rogue traders exist and projects do go wrong. However, for every rogue there is a skilled, experienced and trustworthy builder who would do an excellent job of building your extension. How do you sort the good from the bad? Well, you can start by triangulating a shortlist of good builders.

**You want to receive three quality quotations for your extension. And because not all builders will follow through, shortlist five.**

Don't be tempted to overkill with a longer list – five is sufficient. In fact, if done properly, shortlisting five will be an achievement in itself.

Triangulation is used in the industry to increase the credibility and validity of data, and the more credible the data, the more trustworthy it is. The way to triangulate a shortlist of good builders for your project is to have them come recommended, accredited and with a fresh and relevant social feed. And the more boxes you can tick, the more trustworthy the data.

Note: Now is not the time to carry out full due diligence – that will come once you've had your quotes in. Right now, the focus needs to be on weeding out potential rogues by triple-filtering the candidates that make it onto your list. Essentially, the mission is to make sure their stories check out across different sources.

You may wish to recall the builders you spoke to when you were initially deciding whether to extend. Providing they tick these three boxes, there is no reason they shouldn't make it onto your shortlist.

### 1. Recommendations

There is no better place to start than by asking for a recommendation. It is very reassuring when someone you know has already used a builder and has a positive experience to share.

A word-of-mouth referral from someone you know is the best, because making an introduction requires effort from the person referring. Otherwise, shoutouts via Facebook or neighbourhood apps like Nextdoor, WeAlert and OLIO are also a fair place to start. Your architect is also a valuable source of recommendations, as they may have worked with builders with the right skill sets for your project type. And who better to recommend than the person in charge of designing the scheme?

The power of a referral lies in being connected by a third party, as it provides an extra, unspoken layer of accountability as well as a point of mutual recourse, should it later be required.

A caveat of caution: marketing agencies have monetised the power of referrals by setting up 'accreditation' websites (more on this later). It is vital to ensure the validity of any referrals you receive, which you can do by ticking off the next two considerations.

## 2. Accreditations

You can expect to see a professional builder accredited by the appropriate industry bodies.

If you run a search on accrediting bodies, the returned results will number into the tens of pages. And it can be impossible to tell the credible bodies from the marketing websites, or the relevant bodies from the ones that cater for larger-scale contractors.

The home improvement and renovation sector benefits from several industry bodies of worthy repute. Two such accrediting bodies are the Federation of Master Builders (FMB) and Which? Trusted Traders. The FMB – a non-profit industry body, established in 1914 – is the foremost representative of the classic residential builder, i.e. the type you need for your extension. They are a voice for the industry, educating and keeping their members informed of latest developments, giving you vital extra assurance. The FMB also offers dispute resolution for its members' customers.

The much-loved consumer body Which? also has an accreditation scheme to protect consumers from rogue traders. Their Trusted Traders scheme gives homeowners real confidence that they are dealing with bona fide and well-established businesses. Becoming a Trusted Trader is a deliberately burdensome process, where Trading Standards are sent in to inspect a prospective member's place of work, years-old invoice records are checked, past and present clients and suppliers are called upon to give references, and more. Builders who are accepted onto the scheme have earned their place on it. Which? also serves as a customer review repository.

Getting accredited takes patience and effort, so when a builder is a member of more than one scheme, it goes a fair way in demonstrating the pride and earnestness with which they ply their trade

## 3. Social feeds

Check out the candidates across their social platforms. The digital sphere has grown beyond Facebook and Twitter, although these are still great for a nosey. Hit up the builder you're considering on Instagram, Pinterest, TikTok, LinkedIn, YouTube, Reddit, Snapchat, Vero and/or whatever the hottest platform is whilst you are looking for builders.

You are *not* looking for glossy photos of their latest project, because these pictures could have come from anywhere and/or been edited.

You *are* looking for are two things:

1. **Consistency**
   Look at whether the prospective builder's messaging is the same across the website and across the aforementioned platforms they have an account on. If they've just gained an accreditation, are they shouting about it on LinkedIn? If they say they have a large team, do you see them hammering away on Insta?

2. **What else is going on in a post**
   On the latest Facebook post, was the worksite tidy or was Maccy D's packaging strewn across the floor? Were the tradesmen dressed suitably for site work or walking about bare-chested? Often what you see in the background is the most telling.

> The way to shortlist good builders for your project is to triangulate your research using recommendations, accreditations and social feeds. Doing so will give you credible insights to help you suss out whether a builder is worth pursuing for a quote.
>
> Shortlist five and prioritise the list, with your favourite (so far) at the top. Then have the top available three come over to quote.

# BUILDER MARKETING TRAPS TO AVOID

Before inviting the top three builders from your shortlist over to quote, you should be aware of some potential marketing traps that could confuzzle an unsuspecting homeowner: find-a-builder sites, quotation websites and customer reviews. Some of these considerations have already been mentioned; however, their importance is deserving of further conversation.

## Find-a-builder websites (and apps)

These types of platforms have exploded in popularity in recent years because they provide homeowners with a convenient shop window to look for builders. Pair this with the single biggest anxiety homeowners have about hiring builders – whether they are letting someone trustworthy into their home – and you have yourself a potent combo.

The secret source of find-a-builder sites is the credibility factor. They give their clients (traders) professionally designed membership logos to use on their vans, clothes, cards and online, as well as space on their platform to showcase their work and post reviews. They look like bona fide, certified, industry-representative bodies, but readers should be mindful that they are for-profit companies that spend fortunes on broadcast, print, radio and digital advertising, in order to get your eyeballs on their website and new members through the door.

However, the barriers for signing up are low, and it's not impossible for traders to use flaky references, feign reviews, or screenshot someone else's sexy interiors to include in their online portfolio. These types of sites can serve a genuine and valuable purpose in helping traders establish an online presence, but it's useful to know about their comparative shortcomings when searching for builders for your project.

## Quotation websites

The appeal of quotation websites is the speed at which they return results. We consumers have grown accustomed to getting the information we seek right away, wherever we are, at any hour of the day. Anything less is considered frustratingly slow. Quotation websites understand this need for speed and cater for it.

Such sites are hyper-optimised to be found first, paying big money to appear at the top of search listings for consumers looking for instant online building quotes. And the business model is devastatingly effective. By punching in search terms like 'get building quote', 'estimated cost of

…', homeowners (who hadn't the prescience to purchase this book) are in effect raising their hands and identifying themselves as customers who want information quickly. Quotation websites give you what you want in exchange for your personal and property information – name, location, property type, project type, urgency, budget and other data points.

Here's the thing, though: the information they spit out is incomplete and out of date and therefore misleading. It simply isn't possible to provide an accurate quotation without physically assessing the nuances of the building or without an accurate design brief … Fact. The project cost information provided serves as a hook to get you in front of their fee-paying clients – tradesmen and builders – for whom the quotation websites are paid-for lead-generation engines. They turn you into a fat juicy commodity for consumption by the industry.

## Customer reviews

Humans are social animals. We like to be in the company of others like us, amongst people with whom we share interests. If others like us are doing something, we are open to doing the same. If people similar to us have something, we tend to want to have it too. And naturally, when people like us know something, we tend to listen to what they have to say. Robert Cialdini was the first to name this phenomenon, which he called social proofing in his book The Psychology of Persuasion. In social proofing, people will follow the actions of the masses, believing that if lots of people are doing something, it must be right.

That's the power of customer reviews.

Reviews give homeowners the foresight of knowing a bit about a person even before they meet them. This breeds familiarity, and familiarity breeds confidence. For that reason, genuine customer reviews are fantastic for both homeowners and builders.

Sounds great in theory … except reviews can of course be fabricated. There is in fact very little to stop anyone from faking a review. Genuine online review sites, find-a-trader platforms and quotation websites provide a very useful repository of client reviews. However, it is up to the homeowner to check the source and sincerity of any such information. A review is only useful if it can be verified in the real world.

Find-a-builder sites, quotation websites and online reviews can all be legitimate platforms that help builders and traders market themselves, but they can all be leveraged for abuse by the unscrupulous. Their success in subterfuge comes from the glossy sheen they give builders' online presence, so always check the provenance of the information they are providing, or you will risk falling into a marketing trap.

# GETTING QUOTES FOR YOUR EXTENSION

Okay, so you've shortlisted five quality builders and prioritised them in order of preference thus far. From this shortlist, some will not be available to quote, for one reason or other, and by the end you will want in your hand three quotations – no more no less. Three gives you a realistic sight of where the market's at. Now comes the time to invite the builders over to provide a quotation.

A builder's home visit can provide a profusion of information ... if you know what to look out for. In fact, the in-person visit is more revealing than the quote itself and should go a long way to informing your decision on whom to hire.

Here is a useful list of things to look out for when a builder comes to visit and helpful questions to ask. The trick to squeezing the most out of this vital stage is to be consistent in what you look for and what you ask of each visiting builder.

## Things to look out for when a builder comes to quote for your project

1. Did your call go through to the builder directly or to an office or virtual assistant?
2. What impression did you get of them on the first call? Were they friendly? Rushed? Brusque?
3. Did your initial call follow a noticeable fact-finding structure, or was it more casual?
4. Did the builder ask you to send across the plans in advance of the visit?
5. Was booking a site appointment straightforward, or was there a lot of toing and froing?
6. Did they arrive on time?
7. What was your first impression when you opened the door?
8. Did they offer to remove or cover their shoes before entering?
9. Did they pull up in a liveried vehicle?
10. How were they dressed and generally presented?
11. How was their body language and overall demeanour?
12. Did they speak more or listen more?
13. Did they ask insightful questions?

14. Did they measure stuff, open access hatches and ask to see the location of utilities?
15. Were they taking notes and pictures?
16. Did they offer up a quote verbally then and there?
17. Did they voluntarily offer to show you past and present work?

You can discern the tangible or intuitive value of each response yourself, and the results will help you form an opinion of the candidate, alongside the actual quotation when you get it.

In addition to the above, here are some helpful questions to ask as part of your fact-find when the builder comes to visit. There will be time for fuller due diligence on the company and the quote later. For now, these questions are to help you gain further insights into the builder's setup.

## Useful questions to ask a builder when they come over to quote

1. Are you familiar with this area?
2. Are you busy at the moment?
3. Are these a good set of plans, in your experience?
4. Are you okay to speak with the architect or engineer directly if you spot any issues on the drawings?
5. Do you use subcontractors / external contractors, or are your team employed by you?
6. Are you hands-on yourself, or do you manage the team?
7. Will you be working to a set schedule?
8. Will all payments be made directly to you?
9. Will there be a team on my job from start to finish?
10. What measures will you take to protect the areas of the home unaffected by works?
11. When would you be available to start?
12. How is your pipeline looking for the next 12 months?

Now you know some of the key things to look out for and are armed with some insightful questions to ask when getting builders' quotes for your project. So that you are best able to compare, it is very important to be consistent with what you look out for and what you ask.

Next we'll take a closer look at the actual quotations builders will provide.

# WHAT TO LOOK OUT FOR IN A BUILDING QUOTE

Now you have shortlisted your preferred builders and received quotes from your top three, let's spend a moment on what you should be looking out for in builders' quotes.

Note: This is not about carrying out due diligence or specific contractual arrangements (that's to come) but about what you should expect to see on a good-quality quotation.

> **Coupled with a site visit, your fully specified working drawings will be sufficient information for the prospective builders to provide a quotation for works.**

Some architects prefer to take job detailing one step further by producing a tender document, tabulating job specifics and providing a set template for builders to price up within, but this is perhaps overkill for more straightforward extension-type projects.

Every winning quotation should contain certain key information. Every quote should fulfil the following points.

## Be binding

The price provided must be a quotation, not an estimate.

An estimate *(or ballpark)* is an approximation of what the job could cost, whereas a quotation is a fixed figure of what the job will cost.

## Be referenced with supporting documentation

This is where you reap the benefits of the hard work and effort put into producing a set of drawings that are planning-approved, structurally sound, compliant and fully specified.

The quotation should reference the planning-level drawings, structural calculations and plan, building regulation drawings and working drawings. In doing so, the plans essentially become the deliverable.

Other supporting documents may include externally supplied items such as kitchens, bathrooms, cupboards, etc, if the builder is responsible for fitting them.

## Be specific in what's included

In addition to delivering the approved plans to the specifications provided, the quotation should also be clear about what else is in scope.

Typically, additional inclusions will be drawn from one of three categories:

1. **Preliminary items**
   These are things that need to happen or to be in place beforehand, to facilitate works. Examples include the provision of skips, welfare facilities, scaffolding, hoarding, and health safety.

2. **Ancillary works**
   These are supporting activities required to enable planned works to proceed smoothly. To give you a flavour: ancillary works may include demolition, waste removal, upgrades to common parts of flats, and heating system adjustments.

3. **Additional works**
   These are items you may wish for in addition to the extension and which are not specified on your drawings, like garden landscaping, decorating, fitting blinds, and so on.

## Be specific on what's excluded

On the flipside, the quote should be explicit on what is excluded.

It is good practice to ask for any exclusions to be priced separately at this stage, because if you later decide to go ahead with any of them, you will at least have agreed the price from the outset, when the builder is incentivised to price competitively to win the work.

It's useful to have a day rate from the builder for 'bitty' ad hoc work that may not lend itself to a fixed price.

In addition to the exclusions, it's useful to have a list of client purchases summarised on the quote, to make it easier for you to budget for those. Client purchases include items like kitchens, bathrooms and finished flooring, to name only a few.

## List any assumptions

If the builder has made any working assumptions that inform the quote, they should be listed.

Assumptions would be made in circumstances where the supplied plans and/or site visit leave a blind spot in the builder's knowledge of the project ahead. Assumptions typically coalesce around things that could not physically eyeballed by the architect, engineer or builder, such as which direction the joists run or the state of electrical–mechanical services within walls.

During times of supply chain volatility, where material prices fluctuate daily, it would not be unreasonable to see assumptions made on the cost of building materials.

By listing assumptions in the quote, both you and the builder have an explanatory baseline for any unforeseen works that may come to pass once the project is underway.

## Give a clear price

The project price should appear full, clear, fixed and unambiguous.

The quote should be priced to deliver the specified project and not priced on the builders' day rate (the latter lending itself to abuse by the unscrupulous).

The quote should state if VAT is non-applicable, included or excluded.

Much debate is given to whether the price should be itemised, broken down by activity, and/or split between labour and material. This should really be left to the builder to present according to their own system. Ultimately, what matters most is how much it costs to deliver a project according to specifications, and you can always drill down on specific costings with follow-up questions.

## Give service-level terms

These will be bound up in the works contract between you and your selected builder anyway, but it is still reasonable to expect the quotation to give reference to important service-level information such as the contract type (more on this later), job duration, working hours, snagging procedure, guarantees, insurance payment schedule and any retention payments.

> Armed with this knowledge, you are now ready to cross-examine your preferred builder by carrying out your due diligence before making the hire.

# DUE DILIGENCE CHECKLIST WHEN HIRING A BUILDER

Now that you've had the quotes back, it is almost time to hire a builder for your extension. Almost.

> **It is incumbent on you to carry out the necessary due diligence on your preferred builder, to make sure that everything you've seen, heard and read thus far checks out, before you go ahead and make the hire.**

There is a lot at stake here. You'll be spending a lot of money on (probably) your most valuable asset and opening up your home to strangers, so it's important that you know what you need to about the person/company in whom you will soon place your trust. In this context, due diligence refers to fact-checking, asking the appropriate questions, and generally doing your homework on the prospective builder.

Use this due diligence checklist before hiring a builder:

1. **Raise queries**
   Ask all reasonable questions about the quotation and get responses in writing. Where appropriate, receive an updated quote and/or contract.
2. **Check client reviews**
   Pick an online review written on any platform, and ask the builder to talk about the project. Better still, email the reviewer and request a reference.
3. **Website spot check**
   Pick one or two points made on the builder's website and ask them to explain a little further, perhaps on core values, on how they work, or maybe about something tucked away in their FAQs. Doing so will stimulate an insightful response and demonstrate that you have your wits about you.
4. **Visit at least one past project – preferably one similar to your own**
   Visit without the builder present so you are free to make probing enquiries. Where possible, also visit a work in progress to get a feel for how the team work on site.
5. **Company status**
   This should be checked at Companies House, to ensure the company is active and trading.

6. **Check the VAT status of the builder**
At the time of writing, the threshold for compulsory VAT registration in the UK is £85,000, which is about one – possibly two – extensions. It's therefore difficult to see how a builder could avoid registering for VAT if they are active and even moderately successful in their craft.

7. **Check any guarantees and warranties offered**
Ensure you know exactly what these cover and if they are insurance-backed. Non-insurance-backed guarantees and warranties are worth only the paper they're written on.

8. **Health and safety paperwork**
Your building company must comply with the Construction (Design and Management) Regulations 2015 (CDM 2015). Ask to see a copy of the builder's health and safety policy, method statement and risk assessment.

9. **Accreditations**
Accreditations like those from Gas Safe, NICEIC, FMB, Which?, HETAS, CHAS and FENSA can and should be easily checked on the relevant bodies' websites.

10. **View the insurance schedule**
Public liability insurance (often referred to as contractor's insurance) is a must. This should provide sufficient coverage and be valid through to at least the end of the project. In addition, if the company is providing any design input, they will need professional indemnity insurance to boot.

11. **Enquire about future work**
The absence of pipeline projects after yours isn't necessarily a negative, but good-quality builders are usually in demand. On the flip side, you don't want an overly busy workbook to detriment the quality of your build.

12. **A formal contract**
This must be in place to sanctify your agreement to pay the builder X and the builder's agreement to provide you with Y.

This 12-point due diligence checklist will help ensure that you know everything relevant and necessary about your prospective building company. If they don't fully tick every point on the due diligence checklist, it's not automatically a showstopper. There is such a thing as knowing too much – if you look hard enough, you will certainly find one reason or other not to make the hire.

Nobody is perfect and no career journey straightforward, so you'd perhaps do well to hit the bullseye on all these points. But if you have followed the process without deviation thus far, you will have mitigated risks and developed a decent all-round picture of the builder, which will hopefully see you right.

# BUILDING WORK CONTRACTS

Now that you've checked out your preferred builder more thoroughly, you are almost ready to make the hire. Almost.

> **Before proceeding, you need to see, understand and be comfortable entering into a works contract with your builder.**

Here's what you need to know about building work contracts. It isn't legal chapter and verse, but rather what the average homeowner needs to be aware of when entering into a building works contract.

Note: Legal advice should always be sought from a qualified professional.

## Entering into a written contract

There is no law stating that a written contract must be in place between you and the builder when embarking upon your home extension. In fact, the contract comes into being the moment you and the builder commit with a verbal agreement. However, it is always best practice to have a written contract in place, with no exceptions.

A contract is a promise or set of promises enforceable by law. By signing into a written contract, both you and the builder are explicitly acknowledging the responsibilities and obligations you have to one another, and writing out the terms of the agreement avoids doubts about what the other expects.

## What a building work contract should cover

Expectations and agreements have already been put down on paper to a large degree, in the form of the architectural drawings and the builder's quotation. There will be a level of repetition between these documents and the contract, but that is fine.

A building work contract should contain the following.

### Project scope

The scope defines what will be delivered as part of the project. In the contract this will only be a headline, and the full ins and outs will be detailed in the quotation (which, as we see under 'Supporting documents' below, is also covered by the contract).

### Contract sum

The total amount you agree to pay for the work, specifying with or without VAT.

### Job duration

When works will start, when works will end, and how to deal with delays. Ideally, the project should be planned to run continuously from start to finish.

### Payment schedule

What you will pay and when. It is advisable that payments are made upon completion of pre-agreed milestones rather than being time-bound. Bank transfers and debit and credit cards are definitely the recommended methods of payment, although some builders still prefer cash. This is okay so long as payments received are signed for by the builder. The payment schedule will also specify the level of deposit required by the builder (a small nominal sum is advisable as it serves as a psychological lock-in to both parties) and the level of retention fee to be held by the homeowner. The payment schedule is negotiable but should be kept fair for both parties.

### Defects liability period

This is the period in which the builder agrees to return to put broken or malfunctioning occurrences right, at no cost. For an extension, one to six months is typical, tying in with the retention fee, which the homeowner should release at the end of the agreed defects liability period. The larger the project, the longer the defects liability period should be.

### Operational arrangements

Working hours, storage of materials, any site-access restrictions, tidying up, designated 'quiet' hours, and any special conditions imposed by a party wall award will be clearly set out.

### Subcontractors and contractors

If subcontractors are to be used, your builder becomes principal contractor and must retain overall responsibility for what is produced as well as the responsibility to fulfil their construction industry scheme (CIS) obligations. Where outside contractors are brought in to perform a specialist task, they are ultimately responsible to you; and as such, you should carry out due diligence prior to awarding the work. In fact, it is likely that you will have a separate contractual agreement directly with outside contractors anyway.

### Supporting documents

Any documents contributing to the delivery of the project should be referenced in the contract so they enjoy the protections laid out in the agreement. These documents typically include the full suite of architectural outputs and drawings, the quotation, any warranty or guarantee offered by the builder, questions and answers captured on email, and any party wall awards where special conditions are agreed. Importantly, the change order sheet should also be referenced (we will meet this document again later).

### Termination

The contract sets out the circumstances and procedures by which either the homeowner or builder may be permitted to end the contract.

## Types of building work contracts

A building contract will either be an off-the-shelf document, or a bespoke contract produced by the builder.

The most prevalent off-the-shelf contracts are those available from the Joint Contracts Tribunal (JCT), the FMB and the RIBA. Each of these bodies serves the purpose of giving legal consecration to the agreement between you (who agrees to pay X) and the builder (who agrees to provide Y). As you would imagine, all are generally worded to cover a ranging level of work, but they are available in derivative forms covering different types of work. You simply pick the one that most closely matches your project.

Alternatively, some builders may opt to provide you with a bespoke contract, which is no less valid from a legal stance. There may be a perfectly good reason why the builder went to the expense and effort of creating a fresh contract from scratch, but it's important you understand what it contains. If in doubt, ask to revert to one of the above off-the-shelf contracts, which you can be confident are fair and balanced for both parties.

## Who administers the building work contract

You have two options here. You can either have your architect administer the contract, or you can do so yourself, directly with the builder.

RIBA-accredited architects are trained in how to run contracts. The benefit of architect-administration is that the architect remains in the loop during the building phase, and some homeowners take comfort in having them retained as go-between. Part of this administration may also include providing work-progress feedback, against which you release stage payments to the builder. This will come with a price tag, however, and the architect will be doing what you could otherwise do for yourself.

Off-the-shelf contracts, particularly those bearing the Plain English Crystal Mark, are easy enough to comprehend and are recognised across the industry.

The ultimate value of a contract lies in the text therein rather than who oversees the signing of it, so only opt for the architect-administered option if it brings you extra peace of mind, rather than for any perceived added material value.

**Building work contracts exist to protect both the builder and homeowner, so all extension projects should have one. If the builder resists entering into a contract, walk away.**

Always read and understand the contract and know what you are signing.

Ask questions and make amendments to the content if necessary.

With that said, you are now all set to go ahead and hire a builder for your house extension.

# STAGE 8: BEFORE WORK STARTS

## BEFORE WORK STARTS – IN A NUTSHELL

All the legwork in finding and hiring the right builder is done, and the site-ready plans are in place. You are almost ready to start work.

Before the vans rock up, you need to have agreed a fair payment schedule that works for both you and the builder. You also need to have readied your home to receive a building crew, together with their plumage of construction kit.

Knowing exactly what to expect at the start of the project will help in setting realistic expectations for the weeks ahead.

# AGREEING A FAIR PAYMENT SCHEDULE

The payment schedule will form part of the contract, but I need to provide dedicated commentary to this important topic.

A common source of friction on contracts between homeowner and builder is the timetable to which stage payments are made. Agreeing a fair payment schedule with your builder before work starts is therefore essential for you both in making the construction phase a success.

There is often an innate tension between homeowner and builder when it comes to payments. Homeowners generally prefer to pay in arrears for work completed, whereas builders like to be paid ahead of time so as not to find themselves out of pocket. However, construction is a service-based industry, and this fact should bear out on the payment schedule, albeit in a manner fair to the builder too.

Builder payment schedules are a polemic issue and, depending on the nature of the project, the scheduling options can be numerous. It's therefore not appropriate to offer up a one-size-fits-all template as absolute. It's perhaps more sensible to table a suggested schedule for a popular extension type, as a basis for discussion between homeowner and builder, and allow both to arrive at a mutually acceptable arrangement.

Although different project types have distinctive milestones, the base logic and structure should be similar across the range of extension types.

Let's look under the bonnet.

## The deposit payment

The deposit should be paid upon agreement to proceed – typically upon signing the works contract. This gives security to both parties that the job will start on the agreed date and allow both to prepare for the start as necessary.

In our example above, the deposit is set at a nominal 1%. Builders would no doubt like a higher figure, but by this stage a homeowner is already invested to proceed, and a contract will already be signed to provide further surety. The 1% is there to serve as a psychological lock-in to both homeowner and builder that the job is going ahead.

## The first real-stage payment

In our example above, this is stage payment 2 – the completion of opening-up works.

By this point in the project, your builder will have already incurred costs in setting up site, ordering the first tranche of material and the labour to open up the roof. Therefore, as the homeowner, you are already ahead of the curve and the builder now working in arrears. Some of these costs will be out-of-pocket expenses, with the builder paying for items on delivery, some using their supplier credit facilities.

Now that you're a few days into the job and you can tangibly account for where expense has been incurred, 10% is a fair first payment.

## Halfway payment

Not surprisingly, this is paid out around the halfway point through the build schedule. That means when the structure is now up and watertight. In the payment-schedule example on the following page, you will see three lots of larger 20% payments from in the early and middle stages of the build, which are in line with the bulky material purchasing.

After that, payment sizes start tapering off.

## The final payment

The final payment on the main sequence falls due upon successful completion of snagging.

Again, builders would prefer for a smaller percentage to be held till the end, but the sum should be sufficiently chunky to keep the team motivated to finish the job well.

By virtue of working towards a finite snagging list, the homeowner gets the quality they expect, and the builder cannot be held to ransom with ever-growing add-ons.

## The retention payment

This is a pre-agreed sum held back by the homeowner for a set period after the practical completion of works.

Industry retention periods range from 3 to 12 months, but for a residential extension, I suggest a retention period of four weeks. This is fairer for the builder, who has by now handed back your extended home, fully snagged. Four weeks allows ample opportunity to start using the new space in the intended way and for any teething issues to surface. Some would argue that it can take months for latent defects (such as settling cracks) to appear, but these are not in the builder's power to control, and it's therefore unfair for their earnings to be held back. Moreover, a retention sum of 2% is sufficient. A homeowner would naturally want to retain more, but again, the extension is complete (and snagged), so the builder shouldn't be penalised by having large sums of money stuck on a job they have already completed.

Additionally, look closely at the payment schedule example below, and you will notice the size of payments tapering off in the final third of the project stages. This is because a majority of bulk-material purchasing (steels, aggregates, concrete, insulation, etc) happens in the earlier stages of the project, and towards the end of the build, the labour element constitutes the builder's largest outlay.

Consider this basic example of a payment schedule for an attic conversion:

| Payment | Milestone | % |
|---|---|---|
| 1 | Deposit | 1 |
| 2 | Completion of opening-up works | 10 |
| 3 | Completion of steel installation | 20 |
| 4 | Completion of timber framing + roofing | 20 |
| 5 | Completion of first fix | 20 |
| 6 | Completion of second fix | 15 |
| 7 | Completion of snagging | 12 |
| 8 | Four-week retention | 2 |
| | Total | 100 |

**A fair payment schedule needs to be equitable for both homeowner and builder.**

Linking payments to productivity gives the builder surety to request payment when a milestone is reached, and the homeowner the confidence to release monies against progress they can physically see being made.

Do not be tempted to arbitrarily link payments to time (i.e. equal payments spread out over the anticipated job duration) just because it makes the project easier to budget for. Doing so leaves the door open for an unscrupulous trader to request payment for the simple act of turning up to site, irrespective of how much progress has been made on the job.

Agreeing a fair payment schedule with your builder is a fundamental component of any successful project. Naturally, homeowners crave the comfort of a schedule skewed in their favour, and the builder seeks protection from being out of pocket, so the agreed payment schedule will need to be a meeting of minds.

The previous house extension stages of finding and engaging with contractors will have gone a long way to establishing trust with your builder, and this is important – without an element of trust that each party will uphold their end of the bargain, the payment schedule could become a stumbling block in the process.

Intermediaries like a clerk of works or your architect could serve in an escrow role, but for a typical residential extension, that might be overkill.

# PRELIMS FOR YOUR EXTENSION

Prelims (short for preliminaries) in construction are the costs associated with running the project, outside of labour and materials. Prelims are a miscellaneous assortment of items, and it is useful to know which ones could affect your project, because you will ultimately be paying for them.

Some builders explicitly reference prelims as part of their quote, whilst others absorb them within the overall price. Either way, the prelims to be aware of for your extension will be one of two types.

## 1. Administrative

If the building company is a larger outfit, they may allocate a project manager to oversee the build, and this management fee might be designated as a prelim. The same is also possible if the builder used a quantity surveyor to price the job during the quotation stage.

The CDM 2015 regulations set out the health and safety responsibilities for domestic projects, but the full suite of requirements probably won't apply to your project, on account of there being fewer than 20 workers on site. However, the builder may carry over some health and safety elements and list them as preliminary items, such as the production of a risk assessment and various building method statements. If the builder offers an insurance-backed structural warranty, the insurance premium for this may also be passed to you as a prelim. Additionally, some builders may opt to recoup time spent sourcing materials as a procurement cost.

## 2. Site-related

Chief amongst site-related prelims are the costs associated with setting up the building site so it's ready to work in. Site setup costs include perimeter hoarding and scaffolding, and security disbursements like a temporary alarm system or keypad site entry.

If a temporary kitchen or bathroom needs to be established because the main ones are out of commission during the build, these might also be classed as prelims. As would the cost of waste disposal – predominantly skips; and possibly wait-and-load waste clearance if you live in a more built-up area, where the cost of a parking bay suspension to accommodate a skip is prohibitively dear.

Welfare facilities and health and safety equipment/clothing are also classified as site-related prelims, as is plant hire (mini diggers, kango drills, safety platforms and other such equipment). Another would be setting out, which involves staking the ground, sometimes by a professional surveyor, to transfer the parameters from the plan into the building site so that walls are built in the right place. Water and electricity may also be attributed as prelims, as could site decommissioning and end-of-job cleaning.

> Now you know a little more about prelims in construction and how they apply to your extension. They may or may not be made explicit in the quotation or contract, but many of them will make an appearance during the quotation and physical build stage.

# HOW TO PREPARE FOR BUILDING WORK

Take this window of opportunity between signing the works contract and before the build begins, to ready yourself and your home to ensure it starts with minimum fuss.

To help you along, here's some advice on how to prepare for building work, split into three categories.

## 1. Outdoor preparation

With outdoor prep, there will be a level of overlap between what homeowners and builders do, so be sure to discuss this before work starts in earnest.

### Safe storage

Although not essential, where possible make space in the garage to allow for the safe storage of materials. You may, for instance, find that your new bathroom arrives ahead of time, and you need somewhere to store it out of the way to avoid damage.

### Parking permit

If you live in a parking control zone, it is incumbent upon you to provide one parking permit for the builder's main vehicle. In some local authorities, parking dispensation may be the more economical option.

### Make way for the skip

If the skip is going onto your drive, move your car out and ask the builder to leave you two scaffold boards to place under the skip to save the driveway from scuffs. If it is going on the road, hold the spot in front (or as close to the front as possible) of your home the day before. If the nearest spot is a way down the road, the builder is entitled to ask for a supplementary fee to account for the additional manpower for waste disposal. The skip permit will be supplied by the skip company, but if you live in a controlled parking zone, check with the council highways department whether an additional parking bay suspension is required.

### Prepare for scaffolding

Clear a path between the front and rear of the house for the scaffolders, and keep the one-metre perimeter around the house unobstructed for the scaffold footings. Where side access is not possible, the scaffold may need to go through the house or require access via the neighbouring garden, so this should be discussed in advance with your builder and consent sought from your neighbour. In the event of footings being placed on a public highway, you will need to obtain an oversail licence from the local authority. This can take weeks to obtain, so check with the highways department ahead of time. The scaffold footings may block side access, so move bins to the front garden.

### Portaloo

Again, this should be discussed in advance with your builder. Ideally, the Portaloo will be placed in the front garden. If it is going on the roadside, be sure to check licensing and citation requirements beforehand with the highways department, as rules differ significantly between councils.

### Relocate media ariels

Scaffolding can interfere with the strength of signals. Have the number of a local TV aerial company on hand in case you need to temporarily relocate the receiver(s) to a new location for the duration of works.

### Temporary cordon

Where works involve building up to a neighbouring boundary, the builder should establish a temporary screened cordon on the neighbour's side, as a barrier between them and the work site. This arrangement will have been pre-agreed during party wall discussions.

## 2. Indoor preparation

As with outdoor preparations, some of the indoor prep will fall in the builder's domain, so talk through the provisions ahead of time.

### Establish temporary amenities

Where your kitchen and/or only bathroom is out of commission because of works, you will need to establish temporary amenities elsewhere in the house, such as a small plumbed-in kitchen in the living room. The same goes for the heating system, the components of which may need to be temporarily relocated or upgraded to facilitate works.

### Clear an access route

Walk the path through your house that the tradesmen will use, travelling through the hallways and up the stairs. As you do, remove items of furniture along the path, including photos from walls, and find ways to protect low-hanging light fittings.

### Protect surfaces

Lay heavy-duty floor protection over the surfaces – fluted polypropylene is ideal, which is made even more effective by double-taping over section joints. If there are rooms you won't be using, turn the radiators off from the valve, lock the door, and line the door edges with masking tape. Window protection film is another good shout. Where scaffolding bridges a roof window or a conservatory, cover the glass with ridged board insulation (or equivalent) to protect against falling objects.

### Make provisions for pets

Your four-legged friends will be impacted by works, particularly by the risk posed from open doors and gates. Consider this impact of works on your pet and make whatever suitable arrangements you see fit.

## 3. Work–life preparation

### Inform your home insurance company

Most insurers will want to know ahead of time of any structural work to your home, so check that the policy won't be invalidated. If it is, your insurers will invite you to take out a supplementary premium for the duration of works.

### Take this opportunity to have a clear-out

As an example, if the action is in the attic, it will need clearing out. Make a trip to the council waste management site for safe disposal, or check in with the builder that it's okay to use the skip when it arrives. And make room in your shed or garage for any household furniture and accoutrements you're keeping that would get in the way of work.

### Give neighbours a heads-up

Let them know when work will be starting and how long it is expected to take. Apologise in advance for any expected disruption and thank them in advance for being so amenable. Courtesy and gratitude go a long way.

### For the first couple of days, work from home and keep your commitments light

Be on hand to help the builders orientate themselves and get familiar with the property (location of stopcocks, heating system controls, etc) and answer questions. And satisfy yourself that adequate surface protection has been provisioned.

### Consider giving your builder a spare key

Admittedly, giving a (partial) stranger the front door key weirds some homeowners out, but doing so is a sensible precaution. On any live building, site accidents can occur. In the event of a mains water leak, power outage or other such emergency, the tradesmen on site should be able to get to the source of the problem to fix it.

## Set your expectations to glamping mode

Accept that, for the duration of works, your home will be a building site – dustier, noisier and colder than you'd otherwise like – and that your diary could be subject to change with little or no warning. Doing this will increase your tolerance for the unexpected and curb anxiety throughout the build phase.

Use this section as a preparation checklist, where the more you tick off, the better prepared you will be for when the building crew arrives on site. You can bypass a lot of this preparatory activity by moving out for the duration or a portion of the works.

Next, let's take a peek behind the curtain on what you can expect to happen when work does get underway.

# WHAT TO EXPECT WHEN BUILDING WORK STARTS

The big day has finally arrived – construction of your extension is about to get underway. But do you know what to expect at the start of building work?

Well, it's not like on TV. Nick Knowles won't be marching a platoon of tradesmen up the street, accompanied by a confetti fanfare. It will be a somewhat gentler affair. You can expect a rolling start over the first one to three days, with the action gradually ramping up as your property transforms from a home to a work–live building site in readiness for works.

It is often the scaffolders who are first on site. They can be a mercurial bunch and quite single-minded in getting the scaffolding up, so it is important your builder is there to meet them and coordinate access where necessary. Of course, if works are limited to ground level, scaffolding won't be required. But site hoarding probably will still be needed, to keep your property safe amidst the constant transit of people and material in and out of your property. Site hoarding may take a couple of days to put up, depending on the site size.

Around the same time, the skip will arrive and be positioned where needed, along with a rubbish chute and safety lights. The Portaloo will also be delivered in the first couple of days. For bigger projects, a site cabin or shipping container may arrive, to serve as the team's resting quarters as well as a clean space for site meetings.

An initial tranche of building material will be delivered. This will be the big stuff – aggregates, timber and steels, etc. It won't be used right away, but builders like to have the material on site so they can crack on without delay when they're ready to use it.

If they haven't already been carried out ahead of the official start date, any ancillary works needed to facilitate the build will also be completed in these first few days. Ancillary works include tasks such as establishing a temporary kitchen, and making heating and plumbing adjustments. Surfaces will also be protected, as previously described.

As these events unfold over the first few days, the build team will gear up to start work in earnest. The first task on the build schedule will be demolition and strip-out work, so be prepared for noise, dust and disruption.

As the homeowner, the best thing you can do to help get the project off to a flyer is to be patient and flexible. Doing so will be much easier now you know what to expect in the first few days.

# STAGE 9: MANAGING THE BUILD

## MANAGING THE BUILD – IN A NUTSHELL

To advise on the technical construction of your extension is beyond the remit of this book. Instead, we will look at a panoply of hints and tips to help you keep on top of the build.

In brief, keep 5% of the build cost as contingency in your back pocket, get all spec changes in writing before agreeing to them, and keep it professional when talking to your builder.

In addition, avoid making the eight crazy mistakes commonly made by homeowners during a project. And if you do find yourself in dispute with Mr Builder, afford him the opportunity to put the mistake right before escalating the matter.

# TOLERANCE AND CONTINGENCY IN CONSTRUCTION

Tolerance and contingency in construction are similar but different concepts. As a homeowner undertaking a house extension, it is handy to know what they are, why they are important and how they specifically relate to you.

## 1. Tolerance

Tolerance in construction is best described as the allowable deviation from the agreed-upon plan. On plan, design software allows for precise measurements, plumb walls, and perfection in the building materials used. On a live building site, however, walls may not sit at exact right angles, and factory-made building materials may arrive on site with dents and dings or have been fabricated a little out of alignment. The potential of such miscalibrations finding their way from the drawing board to your home is a known risk in construction, and so a general tolerance of 5% tolerance should be allowed as a means of mitigating possible disconnects between plan and site.

There are countless real-life scenarios in which mitigating measures might need to be deployed. A few examples:

- Narrowing of window openings to accommodate window casings manufactured a few millimetres too small
- Showerheads that need relocating to avoid ceiling joists
- Kitchen units that need packing out to offset uneven walls
- ACO drains that need repositioning so they line up with the paving slab pattern

Unfortunately, there is no truly practical way to measure what 5% tolerance should look and feel like. Rather, the takeaway message is to welcome a small dose of flexibility to the project as a whole. Doing so could avoid potential scheduling delays and rework costs, and generally make you a little more accepting of minor bumps in the road on the journey to completing your extension.

A contingency is a budgetary amount held in reserve to deal with unexpected circumstances. Again, there are many examples of such circumstances on a building project. For example, during strip:

- You may discover a dry rot affliction to the studwork
- You might come face to face with protected species like bats or badgers

- Tree roots may stretch further into your plot than you had anticipated
- Asbestos could be found lurking in the attic

Whatever the circumstance, it must be dealt with, and that is what the contingency's for. A contingency of somewhere between 10% and 20% is generally considered standard in the industry. However, if you have followed the advice in this book as practicably as possible, your level of preparedness will be higher and chances of encountering the unexpected lower, so a contingency budget of 5% (up to 10% if being cautious) should suffice.

Be careful not to conflate the contingency fund with add-ons or scope creep, wherein you expressly request additional tasks or specification upgrades to the original schedule of work.

> Keeping a 5% tolerance in mind for deviations from the plan will endow you with a psychological cushion that will take the edge off the stress of unexpected obstacles throughout your extension project.
>
> Although it's technically not required, a small contingency for budget overruns will empower you to get on and deal with said obstacles swiftly, if or when they arise.

# HOW TO HANDLE SPECIFICATION CHANGES DURING THE BUILD

Despite best efforts to account for every detail in the run-up to the build phase, it remains likely that at some point during construction, there will be a departure from the designed plan. When there is, you will need a simple and effective way to deal with it. Enter the change order.

Cast your mind back to the start of your home improvement sojourn. You'll have known for certain that you wanted to extend, with perhaps a rough mental image of what the extension may look like. Between then and now, you and your design team have incrementally developed that image through the course of the architectural process, layer by layer, into a fully specified plan, which your builder could pick up and work from, to a contracted price.

However, even the best-laid plans can go a little off piste. This is particularly prescient within the construction industry, where designing and building even a modest extension requires many skills across different disciplines, from the homeowner providing a detailed design brief and the architect getting plans approved in a tricky area, to the engineer calculating the optimal beam arrangement and the tradesmen bringing the theorised design to life. There is a fair chance that somewhere along the chain, something will go awry.

There are five overriding reasons that your extension plan might need to be modified during construction.

## 1. You

Client-led spec changes are perhaps the largest contributing factor, and it is very common indeed for a homeowner to decide one thing during the technical design stage, and then perform a complete volte-face during the build. Examples of client-led spec changes are endless – everything from the location of stud partitions to the placement of the garden tap. This is to some extent understandable – to get a true grasp of the design choice at hand, one often needs to be standing within the physical space itself to appreciate the decision's impact.

## 2. Unexpected (adverse) site conditions

As mentioned before, following the house extension process laid out in this book as closely as possible will minimise the risk of the unexpected occurring. But it won't eliminate it. Just a few examples of the unexpected are the discovery of rising damp, dangerous wiring, insufficient supports to existing openings, or old lead pipes.

## 3. Labour availability and material supply chain issues

These may force a specification change upon you. For instance, it is not uncommon for an order of bifolding doors to be placed weeks ahead of time, only for the product to be stuck in port for weeks on end. Such delays have been magnified ten-fold since Brexit and compounded further by the Covid pandemic.

## 4. Knock-on effects of design errors

Despite every effort by your design team to stay bang on point, there is the possibility that design errors made upstream in the process will meander their way downstream and onto the building site. For example, a miscalculated roof angle; or the discovery of an internal partition thickened over the decades with plaster, where the engineer thought a load-bearing wall to be.

## 5. Accidents

Unfortunate accidents on site could force your hand to make a change. For instance, the receipt of damaged goods critical to the build timeline may demand a workaround.

> **Whatever the reason for the change, the simplest and most effective way to deal with it is a change order document.**

A change order is a mutually agreed variation between the client and builder to the originally contracted price, specification or work schedule of a construction project. Put simply, both you and the builder agree to a specified change in the plans for an agreed price.

The change order document sits in parallel with the existing works contract and payment schedule. On it you record what extra or changed pieces of work the builder has agreed to carry out, and for how much. The change order means the pre-agreed work schedule, contract and quote don't need to be altered every time there is a change to the plan, because all departures from the original are recorded here in real time on the change order. Importantly, this also includes any credited funds you might be due, in circumstances where the change in question means less labour or material spend by the builder. Because all changes are agreed in writing in the change order, they cannot later be disputed by either party.

Even though the change order won't exist at the time of locking into the building contract, it should still be cited as an addendum to the contract.

During works, you will have to come to an agreement with the builder as to when the change order – or part of the change order –will become payable. Again, the document will sit alongside the pre-agreed main payment schedule and not in replacement of it.

That is how to handle specification changes during a building project. Overall, be prepared for some degree of variance on site from what was designed on plan. These changes can be elegantly managed using a change order document to record any agreed amendments.

# HOW TO INTERACT WITH YOUR BUILDER EFFECTIVELY

In earlier chapters I talked about the importance of clear and simple communication between you, your design team and your build team throughout the house extension process.

Here are five interaction best practices that your builder will genuinely appreciate, and which will help construction run that little bit smoother.

## 1. Communication mode

You and your builder will be in regular day-to-day contact. However, for meaningful communication that affects the outcome of the job, it is best to communicate by email rather than text, WhatsApp or other messaging app. Emailing is no more time-consuming from your phone and, importantly, it reinforces the line between the personal and the professional.

Be realistic on response rates, and don't panic if you don't get a response within seconds – builders commonly chunk up email and paperwork to designated times of the day when they aren't in hands-on operation mode.

## 2. Interaction timings

The temptation to share any thoughts as and when you have them will be almost irresistible, but doing so will likely irritate the builder, who wants to get on with the job at hand. It will also cause frustration for you, if you don't get immediate replies to your queries.

Rather than drip-feeding the builder your thoughts, questions and ideas, bundle them up and agree a convenient weekly slot to formally meet the builder on site. Then you will be sure to get responses to questions, and the builder won't begrudge your asking.

Meet during regular working hours. On site that is typically Monday–Friday 08.00–17.00 and Saturdays 08.00–13.00. This might mean you going into work a little later, or leaving a little earlier, but it is incumbent on you as the homeowner to make the time, not for the builder to sacrifice evenings or weekends – they too have life commitments outside of work.

## 3. Get it in writing

Following these regular site meetings, capture any resulting actions or agreements in writing, by email. This is in no way patronising to the builder. In fact, it will help both of you in clarifying understanding of what was discussed and provide the opportunity to correct miscommunications before implementation.

Don't forget, if specification changes have been agreed, your change order should also be updated to reflect this.

## 4. Remain professional

Building projects have a knack of surfacing any of life's underlying issues that were otherwise lying dormant.

The strain on finances, the angst of constant people in your house, moany neighbours, endless decisions, loud machinery, winter draughts and general clutter can be enough to make the most patient of us sour.

However, don't unburden all these woes on the builder, as many clients unfortunately do. Equally, don't be a saint – speak up if there is something bothering you that cannot wait until the next site meeting.

## 5. Set the mood

Most homeowners are surprised to learn this, but it is true that, as the employer, you are the apex authority on site. As such, you wield the power to make the building project a pleasant experience ... or a less agreeable one.

Bar none, happy building sites are created when the principal contractor is in a good mood, and to a large extent everyone else will take their cue from you.

> Follow these communication best practices to help you interact with your builder more effectively during works, and for you both to enjoy a smoother ride to project completion.

# EIGHT CRAZY MISTAKES TO AVOID DURING THE BUILD

As we have seen on our sojourn through the house extension process, the road-to-home improvement glory is littered with potholes, each of which could leave your renovation plans with a nasty, potentially journey-ending puncture.

Forewarned is forearmed, so here are eight common crazy mistakes homeowners make during a building project, and why you should avoid making them.

## 1. Going on holiday

Homeowners will need to find temporary accommodation during works for renovations and extensions where essential amenities (primarily the kitchen and bathroom) are out of bounds, and the prospect of escaping the discomfort of a building site for a fortnight in the sun can be very alluring. It can be even harder for families with school-aged youngsters to relish remaining on site throughout the summer holidays.

Jet off at your peril, however. Despite having planned out the design in the technical phase, you will not get a true feel for the new space until the walls are built, partitions are constructed and you are standing in the middle of it.

In being present, you can satisfy yourself that construction is proceeding as imagined and feel content that the design choices made earlier were the correct ones. And if they are not, you can easily adjust them whilst the work unfolds. Doing this would be markedly more difficult over FaceTime from the Algarve.

## 2. Micromanaging tradesmen

Don't let the pendulum swing too far the other way by hovering over the tradesmen as they work.

One step further are the homeowners who micromanage tradesmen whenever their boss isn't present. And one step further still are those who ask tradesmen to carry out additional unscheduled activities without going directly through the boss.

These are devastatingly proficient ways to annoy your builder by undermining their authority. And you'll slow down project to boot, by confusing workers with mixed messages.

## 3. Procrastinating on important decisions

On occasion, you will need to react to acute situations that arise on site – situations that require a quick response to ensure the project timeline and budget are not impacted.

The scenario could be any number of things, for example bifolding doors that have been manufactured too short, finding yourself one tile short of a complete bathroom, or deciding how to handle the clumps of decades-old plaster dropping off the ceiling.

Whatever the problem, and as inconvenient as it may be, it's likely your builder will need a speedy decision from you to put the fire out. You therefore need to be prepared to take time out when needed and act swiftly.

## 4. Supplying building material

Some homeowners assume that builders add a creamy margin for themselves when purchasing building materials for a project then passing the cost on to the client. As a result, those homeowners offer to purchase materials themselves.

Where it is true that showroom-type suppliers incentivise the trade to refer clients, they do not do so to the financial detriment of the homeowner. In fact, it's quite the opposite – clients are rewarded for their custom with genuine discounts off recommended retail prices as a result of coming through a builder. The primary purpose of a supplier trade account is to allow the builder better cashflow management with the benefit of (typically) 30-day settlement terms.

By offering to supply building materials yourself, you risk undermining your builder, inferring you don't trust them to procure on your behalf. In addition, sourcing and procuring materials is a skill in itself – even everyday building materials have an esoteric lexicon of their own. If you get the order wrong, you will end up paying for your error in time and money.

Finally, getting materials physically on site often comes down to the personal relationship between the contractor and supplier, and those with strong relationships enjoy a less disrupted supply chain.

## 5. Supplying tradesmen

It is not uncommon for a builder to be asked to omit a part – or a whole chunk – of work from the build schedule because the homeowner 'has a mate' in the trade who can do it instead.

Offering to supply your own tradesmen is a magnificent way to irritate the person responsible for delivering your dream extension. Doing so infers the builder is not up to the task (in which case, why did you hire the builder in the first place?), which could quickly dilute the trust between builder and client.

Moreover, having outside tradesmen on site disrupts the team dynamics, and leaves you with the unenviable job of project managing the outsourced piece of work yourself.

## 6. Renegotiating prices

Shockingly, some homeowners try to haggle down the price or cut corners on the build schedule mid-construction, after terms have been agreed and signed. The motivation is usually to cost save, as ill-prepared homeowners come face to face with the financial reality of a building project.

Renegotiating prices is wholly unacceptable. A full and transparent payment schedule, and the list of exclusions to budget for, have been mutually agreed from the outset.

Nothing positive can come from an attempt to renegotiate prices, and many builders would down tools and walk off site at the perceived insult.

## 7. Being a bad payer

To be a bad payer is the manifestation of original sin in the construction industry.

Bad here means paying later than the agreed date, or paying less than the agreed sum.

The payment schedule will have been deliberately devised to keep the project sufficiently cashflowed. Cashflow is the fuel that keeps the engine running, ensuring materials get to site and the building team turn up to work each day. And without receipt of timely monies, project success is at risk.

It is unreasonable to expect the builder to self-fund the job with their own cash in the repeated absence of timely payments, and they have the contractual power to stop work if they choose to. Of all the crazy mistakes homeowners make during a building project, paying badly is the craziest.

## 8. Playing the blame game

Despite best-laid plans, sometimes things go wrong, and external events can impact job progress.

Examples of mishaps are countless. To name only a few: your builder might be called away to deal with an emergency on another job, heavy rain may pour through the temporary roof, the kitchen tiles may be installed incorrectly, the electrician could put a foot through the ceiling, or your driveway might be left scuffed by a hasty skip change.

Whatever the issue, it is important to keep cool and avoid pointing the finger, even when the case appears open and shut. Give your builder the opportunity to notify you of the issue and to fix it. The chances are they'll want it resolved right away to keep the project on track, but going into confrontation mode immediately creates a you-versus-builder scenario, which will not help either of you move past the problem efficiently.

> Now you know eight of the craziest mistakes homeowners make during a building project, you have no excuses if you make the same.
>
> Next up, let's dig a little deeper into the last mistake above – playing the blame game – and learn how best to deal with accidents and mishaps.

# COMMON DISPUTES THAT CAN ARISE ON A BUILDING PROJECT

By following the house extension process laid out in this book as closely as possible, you will have naturally reduced the risk of a home improvement disaster. However, no plan is completely foolproof, so let's consider some of the common disputes that can arise on a building project and how to overcome them.

Note: The advice dispensed in this section is experiential, and professional legal advice should always be sought for issues of consequence.

There are two types of problems: superficial issues and consequential issues.

## 1. Superficial issues

Superficial here refers to the common accidents that might occur during the course of a building project, which do not affect the overall deliverability of your extension but nevertheless need to be rectified.

The most common examples:

- Water damage caused by leaks
- Electrical faults
- Damage to property caused from falling objects, transiting material and/or resulting from the movement of workers to and from site
- Damage caused in the handling of material (sanitary ware, kitchen appliances and such)

The best way to deal with minor mishaps is to alert the builder at the earliest opportunity and in writing. If the problem is acute, it will need immediate attention. If not, it is acceptable for your builder to acknowledge the fault and commit to fixing it at a later, more suitable time, so as not to disrupt the workflow.

## 2. Consequential issues

These are more serious occurrences that, if left unattended, adversely impact the overall deliverability of the extension.

There are four types of consequential issues.

### Substandard work

In addition to the protection you enjoy under the works contract, you are covered by the Consumer Rights Act 2015, whereby a contracted agreement to supply a service must be executed with reasonable skill and care. You can therefore expect the build to be to the level of craftsmanship agreed and constructed with the quality of materials expected. If either falls short, the work can be deemed substandard and could affect overall deliverability.

## Escalating costs

The checks and balances written into the house extension process reduce uncertainty in the system, drastically shrinking the causes for sudden or unforeseen building costs mid-project (aside from force majeure).

Regrettably, low-balling quotes to win work is a favoured tactic of the rogue trader, and once work starts, out come the extras. And these unexpected extras could very well put excessive stress on your budget and halt construction.

## Delays

Your builder may have other projects running in parallel with yours, and on occasion may need to divert manpower from your job to deal with an emergency.

If this happens on the odd occasion and/or for a short period of time, do not panic. However, if your project is regularly left unmanned or insufficiently resourced, this will impact the completion timetable.

Another cause of delays is the late arrival of goods and materials, which is largely out of the contractor's hands. We witnessed, for instance, the UK starved of construction material following Brexit, and before that due to China's insatiable appetite for the raw material fuelling its economic growth.

## Incomplete work

No further explanation's required on this one, but for the avoidance of doubt: incomplete work is when the builder leaves the site without finishing the contracted schedule of work.

Incomplete work may come about as a result of one – or a combination – of the above issues not being (fully) resolved, or due to breach of contractual terms from either party, or even on account of the builder ceasing trading.

> Substandard work, escalating costs, delays and incomplete work are the four most common issues that, if left unattended, could derail your extension.
>
> If you suffer the misfortune of encountering one of these issues, you will need to know how to deal with the situation ...

# OVERCOMING DISPUTES

Whilst it's helpful to understand the common disputes that can arise on a building project, it's vital to know how to overcome them.

The four-step escalation ladder below sets the protocol to follow in dispute resolution.

Effective dispute resolution is about taking the path of least resistance. It's therefore best to work through the following steps in order, escalating to the next level action only if the previous one proves unsuccessful.

Note: Remember to communicate in writing, preferably by email.

## Step 1: Provide the opportunity to put it right

A professional builder knows they are only as good as their last client. They will want to protect their reputation by putting right the mistake, so allow them sufficient time and space to do so. Email them with photos of the issue, with description of works and follow up with a phone call.

Resist the urge to call your builder out on social media. This will immediately put them on the defensive and risk creating a confrontational scenario.

If you find that the issue isn't resolved after this step, provide written forewarning of your intention to escalate the matter.

Proceed to step 2 if the builder has still failed to respond.

## Step 2: Complain to the accrediting body

Presuming you followed the suggested hiring process, your builder will be accredited with one or more reputable trade bodies. These have well-established mechanisms in place to deal with disputes. Therefore, to escalate the issue, raise a complaint and follow the dispute resolution procedure laid out by the accrediting body.

If the accrediting body has adopted an alternative dispute resolution (ADR) scheme, then all the better for all concerned, as it allows for a resolution pathway that avoids the courts, instead using mediation and arbitration. Through this process, your case will be assigned a liaison officer to bridge the communication gap between you and builder. With luck, your builder will want to preserve their reputation within the accrediting body.

In the absence of an accrediting body, contact the Citizens Advice Bureau. The builder is not beholden to the CAB, so the outcome can be hit and miss, but hopefully the prospect of a third party looking in will prompt a positive response.

## Step 3: Letter before action

In step 1 you demonstrated a willingness to communicate amicably, and you continued to do so through step 2 via a third party. If these steps have been unsuccessful, you will need to take a toothier approach. Before hiring a solicitor, however, send the builder a letter before action.

This is a formal communiqué, putting the builder on notice that court proceedings will be brought against them in the event of continued inaction. You could write the letter of action yourself, offering up a final opportunity to resolve the dispute before the matter is formally passed to (named) solicitors, who will take up the case.

By sending this letter, you are again formally ratcheting up the seriousness of the problem, in an attempt to jolt the builder into action. In addition, it would be understandable if you felt the need at this stage to reach out to your builder on social media.

## Step 4: Legal action

By this stage, you have provided the builder with every opportunity to put things right. If they still refuse to resolve the cause of the dispute, it is time to unholster the guns.

Hire a solicitor experienced in domestic construction, and pursue legal action to bring about a resolution.

The solicitor will advise you on their process. But as a general rule: keep all communication in writing throughout all these steps, take photos to evidence the issue, and chronicle interactions as they unfold.

> Even the pursuit of legal action cannot guarantee a positive outcome. I must stress again that the best way to minimise the risk of falling into dispute is to hire a high-quality, professional builder in the first place, using the hiring procedure previously set out.

# STAGE 10: COMPLETION OF BUILDING WORK

## COMPLETION OF BUILDING WORK – IN A NUTSHELL

Even the smoothest of builds can run into choppy waters towards the end of construction. This is when the homeowner's enthusiasm to move in and the builder's eagerness to move on can lead to a lot of loose ends and a shedload of frustration for both parties.

You can avoid befalling this fate with a clear understanding of how to effectively close out your project.

This includes following the recommended snagging protocol, to ensure the finishing work is just as you expect before bidding the team bon voyage.

Finally, offer your builder a gesture of goodwill and end the project on a high.

# CLOSING OUT THE BUILD

The final stages of construction represent a potentially vulnerable point in the client–builder relationship, so it is critical to manage this period well. It is therefore important to know the steps involved in successfully closing out a building project.

Until now, the entire build may have run without any major hiccup, but there is still a risk of events veering off track towards the tail end of proceedings. As enthusiastic as you are to get your house back, the builder will be just as keen to leave for the next job, which can cause both of you to rush and mistakes to happen.

> **The risk of derailment at this stage is compounded by misconceived notions of what constitutes the end of the project, in the minds of both the homeowner and builder.**

Imagine the dissatisfaction of reading a novel though to the end, only to find the final page has been torn out. Similarly, the absence of an ending provokes exasperation with homeowners, who are left craving closure; and frustration for the builder, to whom the project never seems to end.

We can square this circle by giving definitive shape to the end of a building project. Contrary to accepted belief, the end of a building project isn't a single point in time. It happens over four phases, the boxes of which must all be ticked.

## Phase 1: Practical completion

Practical completion is the most obvious phase of closing out a project. It is what people generally take to be the end, marking the moment the house is 'handed back' to the homeowner.

This is when scheduled work is complete, barring any known omission or delays. You'll know practical completion is close when the final building control inspection takes place and when non-essential tradesmen are taken off the job to be reassigned elsewhere.

The builder will have cleaned up and cleared out the site of tools, plant and materials, and (hopefully) will have run through how to use the new installations (door locking mechanism, heating controls, AV app, CCTV, etc).

They may have left site, but they'll return shortly for phase 2.

## Phase 2: Completion of snagging

More on this coming up in the next section, but in summary for now: snagging is the process of identifying and fixing minor defects at the end of a building project.

Upon or shortly after practical completion, you will make a list of items that still need to be completed or fixed, which the builder returns to complete before receiving the final scheduled payment.

Completion of snagging is also a good time to inform your home insurance provider that works are complete.

## Phase 3: Paperwork handover

Ensuring you receive all the relevant project documentation is a crucial part of closing out a building project successfully.

Use the following checklist to ensure you don't miss anything out.

1. Completion certificate, issued directly from building control (this certifies that the extension meets the legal minimum standards)
2. Electrical installation certificate
3. Gas installation certificate (if applicable)
4. HETAS installation certificate (if applicable)
5. FENSA installation certificate (if applicable)
6. Other brand-specific product warranties (such as Topseal roofs or K Rend external rendering)
7. Manuals and warranties for all appliances, fixtures and fittings
8. Insurance-backed structural guarantee from the builder (if offered)
9. Other delivery dockets and receipts

## Phase 4: Payment of retention

The fourth and final phase in closing out a building project successfully is when you release the retention payment.

Before doing so, you will have identified any minor latent defects that have presented since snagging, and the builder will have addressed them.

> Owing to the absence of an industry-wide accepted milestone to mark the end of a build, neither the homeowner nor the builder quite knows what the end should look or feel like, and this can cause frustration all round.
>
> Successfully closing out a building project requires a mindset shift from both parties, to accept that the end of a building project is a mini process on its own. Following the four phases laid out here will help you administer the close effectively.

# HOW TO SNAG EFFECTIVELY

Snagging is an integral part of closing out any building project. You may already be familiar with the term, particularly if you have undergone some sort of building renovation in past. However, to ensure your house extension finishes well, it is imperative that you know exactly what the process involves, so here is a guide to snagging building projects effectively.

## What snagging is

Given the varied nature of construction, there is no universally accepted definition of snagging. In the home renovation and improvement sector, however, we can take snagging to be the process of identifying and fixing minor defects at the end of a building project.

## Types of snags

The snags and defects you may encounter are too numerous and varied to list out completely, so instead I will categorise the seven different types, with a classic example of each.

1. **Design flaws**
   A kitchen cupboard with adjacent doors that clash when fully opened
2. **Materials issues**
   Efflorescence in roof tiles or brickwork
3. **Omissions**
   Anything accidentally missed from the build specification – usually smaller things that happen at the tail end, such as the installation of an external power socket
4. **Craftsmanship**
   An uneven handwash basin that pools water on its flat surface
5. **Functional defects**
   An external door with a misaligned locking mechanism
6. **Cosmetic defects**
   Surface scratches and scuffs
7. **Latent defects**
   Slow-emerging issues that appear after weeks or months, such as setting cracks between the new staircase stringer and adjoining wall. You won't catch these on your snag hunt, but you have the retention payment as your safety net in case such things materialise.

## When to snag

The optimum time to snag is when the job reaches practical completion, i.e. when the builder packs up and leaves site, handing you back your home.

Book a professional post-build clean immediately after the crew depart (or make sure your own clean is thorough) – a clean space will reveal any dents and dings concealed beneath dust.

## How long snagging should take

Following a prompt clean, one to two days provides sufficient opportunity for you to inspect the new space and experience the functionality it provides.

Anything longer than this would be unfair to the builder – they will be keen to see the snagging list so they can plan resources, block out time to carry out remedial work, and get paid.

## Who should do the snagging

In a word: you. You know your expectations and requirements better than anyone, so use the new space in its intended way, jotting down any defects as you encounter them.

You could hire a professional snagging surveyor to do it, but retaining their services for a standalone extension is perhaps excessive (and costly). Their primary products are intrusive surveys, and their primary market is new-build homes.

## How to snag effectively

Effective snagging isn't difficult, but it does require attention to detail. And the best advice for effective snagging is to keep it simple.

Pen and paper are okay, but photos are better. Armed with your camera/phone, start at the very top and work your way down and around. Move systematically, inspecting the ceilings, walls, floors, doors, windows, electrics, plumbing, mechanical aspects (anything with a moving part), and the fixtures and fittings. Also check the parts of the house adjoining the building area for any collateral damage. Check for any of the first six types of defects listed above, from design flaws through to cosmetic defects. If you spot a defect, take a photo, and note down a pithy description.

Snag the whole thing once, then do it again with a fresh pair of eyes. Do it a third or fourth time if necessary.

List out all defects captured on a single document, each with a photo and description. It might be tempting to send the photos straight to your builder after you take them, but don't do this. The act of transposing the defects to a single document will force you to review the snags before they go to the builder, and the better quality your snag sheet, the more thorough the remedial work will be.

There are also several superb apps available that help streamline the snagging process.

## Rectifying snags

Hand the final snagging list over to the builder and agree a mutually convenient date to carry out the remedial work, ideally within a fortnight of practical completion.

To your builder, the snag sheet is a to-do list of tasks that need completing to your satisfaction before receipt of the final instalment of the payment schedule. Although the builder will be returning at the end of the latent defects period to address any slow-emerging issues, any further snags that you flag up after presenting your final snagging list can be treated as chargeable extras, so be sure to snag thoroughly from the outset.

Do not let the builder's enthusiasm to finish the job deter you from being thorough when snagging. The more systematic you are with it now, the less chance there will be you'll need to call the builder back later.

With this mini guide to snagging building projects effectively, you are in a better position to play an active role in helping to bring a successful, strong end to the building work.

Next, let's see how you can finish the project on a high.

# END YOUR BUILDING PROJECT ON A HIGH

By now your builder will have returned at the end of the agreed defects liability period to address any lingering issues before collecting the retention payment. And that's that – the project is finished. Now, there are things you can do to help everyone feel happy during and after the final stages.

This has two major advantages. First, you may well need the builder back for something in the future. Ending on jovial terms begets goodwill, which may prove helpful if you need a helping hand down the line. Second, the team will have worked their socks off constructing your dream extension, and conveying a gesture of gratitude for this is simply a very nice thing to do.

Here are six ways to help you end your building project on a high.

## 1. Be reasonable

You need to be reasonable about releasing the final payment. A builder earns when the job is complete, and the final payment is released only upon satisfactory completion of snagging. Further, the retention is released only at the end of the defects liability period. Therefore, don't keep your builder waiting for the money they have already earned by holding back payments for excessively finicky things. Some rogue homeowners refuse to pay or draw out final payment on spurious grounds, in the hope of saving money or squeezing more work out of the builder for free. Regrettably, this sort of conduct is a known phenomenon in the industry.

## 2. Be patient

Please exercise patience when awaiting additional works. Whilst the trades are on site, homeowners often ask their builder to carry out extra work around the house, as additions to the contracted schedule of work. However, it is likely that the builder will already have lined up the next project and so needs to complete your extension by a specific date, so you might have to wait for the team to return at a later date to tackle the extras. As much as you might want the hallway repainted before unveiling your spanking new extension to the neighbours, please be patient – the builder simply might not be free to do it right away.

## 3. Allow pictures

Give the builder permission to post updates of project progress on their social feed and help them share their craft with a wider audience. Indeed, some may ask to return to take photographs a few weeks after completion, once the new space is fully decorated and furnished, to add those pictures to their project portfolio.

## 4. Make a social media shout-out

Post a picture of your fabulous extension on social media, and credit your design team and builder with a tag and a shout-out. Doing so is free, and you get to show off your home version 2.0 at the same time. If public shares aren't your thing, you could instead offer up your builder's details when someone posts a recommendation request online. Facebook and neighbourhood apps are particularly good for this.

## 5. Give a testimonial

At the end of the job, give a testimonial about your experience. Leaving a review on the builder's preferred social platform or Google listing will be the most helpful form of positive feedback, as reviews endure and proliferate brand exposure. If you are feeling really chuffed with the job, leave a video testimonial.

## 6. Complete the circle

Back when you were shortlisting builders for your extension, you would have (you should have) visited previous projects as part of your due diligence. Now, fresh prospective clients will want to do the same, and allowing a handful to tour your lovely extension would be very welcome. The same applies to serving as a reference, if requested.

> It goes without saying that, if the job went well, you would want to recommend the builder when the natural opportunity to do so arises. Nonetheless, to help ensure that you end the project on a high, implement (at least some of) the suggestions laid out here. Doing so doesn't cost you anything, leaves both parties feeling happier, and may just earn you a quid pro quo for the future.

# CLOSING THOUGHTS

As you race toward the end of the book, there are unwitting homeowners across the UK right now – including in your neighbourhood and on the very road where you live – trooping straight into a home improvement disaster, with bulging wallets in hand and broad smiles slapped across their faces. Ask a neighbour how their extension went, though, listening carefully to their answers, and you will soon discover that home improvement failures are sadly all too common. Not for you, though. By reading this book, you have exponentially increased the chances of extending your home without wrecking it in the process. Congrats.

Construction is a flagship industry for the British economy, but its low barrier to entry makes it an inherently risky marketplace for everyday consumers.

We've identified two leading reasons why so many home renovations end in failure. The first of these is the lack of overall accountability that comes from working in an intrinsically disjointed system. The second is the overemphasis placed on the physical build phase of the project, to the detriment of the tonnes of essential work required before a shovel can hit the ground. More importantly, though, you now also understand that the former can be assuaged by enshrining accountability into an unbiased document (a set of master plans) as far as practically possible, and how the dangers of the latter can be lessened by following the well-tried house extension process proposed. Halleluiah.

Journeying through the house extension process, you have picked up some killer tips that will seriously help you get the most out of each project stage. By the time you are through to the other end, you should have a beautifully planned and well-constructed extension, designed and built by a power team who understood your requirements perfectly, and who delivered on them with minimal deviation or drama.

Every piece of insight shared in this book will in some way add value to your extension project. But if I was forced to offer just one piece of advice that could add the greatest value to your project as well as to the industry as a whole, it would be for homeowners and industry professionals to treat builders with greater deference. Too often, architects, designers, engineers and surveyors kick problems and assumptions down the road for builders to deal with on site. Builders are no more able to solve problems than their colleagues upstream, but they are all too often required to pick up the baton because there is no one else at that stage who will. Furthermore, builders are often given short shrift by the imperious homeowner, who harbours unrealistic expectations as to what things cost. The architectural dictum, function follows form, perfectly captures the point. Ultimately, a builder's work is a reflection of the processes, pressures, demands and incentives of the commercial environment in which they operate.

That is not to say that there aren't rogue builders in the industry. There are many. Our country's decision makers have the power to make the home improvement industry a safer marketplace for consumers. I, alongside others, continue to lobby the government to introduce mandatory licensing of the building industry. In just the same way a gas engineer must be authorised to work by a registration body, builders should be registered and regulated by a governing body, whose role it is to ensure that only suitable persons are permitted to work as licensed builders. The introduction of mandatory licensing would jettison bad apples from the industry and offer consumers greater protection as they embark upon home renovation. The role of this licensing body could then be further developed so it has powers of enforcement for non-compliant members; provide a secure escrow facility for transactions; and offer an industry-wide rating system for its members, to encourage continued professional development. A rising tide lifts all boats; as standards of work would inevitably rise, the industry would benefit, as a genuine connection could be made in the minds of homeowners between quality and cost. Once we have crossed the Rubicon and introduced mandatory licensing, we will look back and consider building without licensing to be as outrageous as driving without a seatbelt.

The construction industry is a broad church. When it comes to industry-level policy making, there is a good deal of common sense in splitting out the homeowner-driven home improvement and renovation sector from commercially driven, large-scale construction. The needs of the two are different; by clumping all of construction in one monolithic block, the needs of the smaller are overlooked, and it is ultimately the consumer who suffers. Divorcing the two, to create a residential building industry and a commercial construction industry, would allow for more sensible, fact-based policy making that is closer to the needs of everyday consumers.

Technology also has a role to play in raising standards in the residential building industry. Building information modelling (BIM) has the potential to massively decrease friction through the design and build process, but it is perhaps too verbose and expensive for 'small' residential deployment right now. As BIM continues to develop, take-up increases and there is certainly scope for a frictionless, easy-to-use, app-based platform in the marketplace.

To close: be confident that you now know what you need to make your extension a shining success.

T.S. Eliot wrote, 'Home is where one starts from.'

To that, I say, 'Start well.'

> If you would like help getting planning permission for your project, hit me up on LinkedIn or speak to the team at architecture100.com.

Printed in Great Britain
by Amazon

35370793R00116